# Terpꝃihori
## A Greek Woman,
## An American Immigrant

A Story of Love, Courage, Hardship and Survival

*By*

Michael George Markulis

Dedicated to my mother, Terpsihori, for giving us a beautiful, full life; to my father, George, for his strength and hard work; and to my brother, John, who has been an inspiration to me all my life, as this story could not have been written without him.

Above all, with my love and admiration, this book is dedicated to my wife, Alicia, who encouraged me to write the story.

Mike G. Markulis

# Contents

# *Foreword*

This is the story of Terpsihori Michael Galanis, who, in 1929, at the age of twenty-one, married a Greek coal miner from the United States of America and left her beloved Greece to seek a new life with her husband in a foreign land. The new life brought her love, a family, and hardship. And yet, despite all the adversity and calamities she faced, she had a beautiful, wonderful, happy life.

This story begins in 1929 when a contractual marriage agreement between the Galanis and Marcoulakis families was established. At the time, Terpsihori Galanis lived in Greece and George Marcoulakis lived in America.

This is a dramatic love story that could have been any young immigrant couple's story. But this story is about two very special people in my life and in the lives of those family members and friends they touched for more than eight decades.

Neither one is with us today. George passed on December 1, 1985, thirty-seven days short of one hundred years old. Terpsihori followed him ten years later at the age of eighty-eight. Not a day goes by that they are not thought of, for they each left a legacy of wonderful stories and memories of what love and family are all about. Theirs was not a fairy-tale life, but a life of hard work, strong religious convictions, and doing the best they could throughout the Depression years. They moved from one coal-mining town to another and from one state to another to do whatever was necessary for themselves and their family. Along the way, they helped others who were in dire need during those difficult times.

Their fifty-six years of marriage resulted in five sons and five beautiful daughters-in-law, who were successful in their own lives and gave Terpsihori and George nine grandchildren and seventeen great-grandchildren. Their legacies have touched each and every one in a special way.

This is Terpsihori's story as told by her number two son, Michael George Markulis, and his memory of the voices of the Markulis' siblings.

Thank you, Mom and Dad, Yaya and Papou. We miss you.

# Introduction

Terpsihori was born on the island of Crete on July 23, 1907, to Michael and Katherine Galanis. She was the eldest of four children. A brother, Nicholas, followed Terpsihori three years later, and then two sisters: Maria, who was five years younger, and then the youngest, Olympia, who was nine years her junior. All three sisters grew up to be beautiful young ladies, bearing a strong resemblance to their mother.

Her father was a very successful and respected citizen in Athens. He was a notary public for the Greek government and had an office in the court house.

Terpsihori, being the first born, was spoiled by her parents. She enjoyed her growing-up years, living in Crete, and moving to Athens and Piraeus, where she went to school. She graduated from high school and was on her way to becoming a school teacher. She was an excellent student, eager to learn and eager to practice her profession, for which she studied so hard.

She was an outgoing, happy young lady who had an appetite for a luxurious good life. She had many friends and relatives to whom she was very close. Little did she know that her life would take a dramatic turn. It seemed that everything happened so quickly for her. In a way, she was excited and, at the same time, apprehensive about the changes that were going to take place. She became aware that her family and another family, the Marcoulakis family from Crete, were arranging a marriage for her to a man who was twenty-one years older.

At that time in Greece many young men were leaving to find work in other countries, preferably in the United Sates. The shortage of men left a void in many cities and towns where there were few young men to marry the girls. Thousands of men left

Greece. A whole generation of young Greek women remained unmarried or had to marry much older men. Many of the men that had immigrated to the United States arranged contract marriages with families in Greece.

Terpsihori had other ideas in mind related to matrimony. She had her eyes on a young Greek closer to her age, and she thought she would eventually marry him. But the arranged marriage with the Greek from the United States was set in concrete, and she was to become the wife of George John Marcoulakis.

The last name Marcoulakis was changed several times over the years. It was changed first to Marcoulis and ultimately to Markulis.

*Terpsihori*

# CHAPTER 1:

# *A Beautiful Wedding*

George was a mature, older man at the age of forty-three. He was considered to be one of the most handsome men from the island of Crete, and the same was true in Carbon County, Utah. With his six-foot frame and muscular build, he looked like a god to Terpsihori. As a young man growing up in Crete and as a coal miner in the United States, George was well known for his strength and athletic prowess. Not knowing anything about George Marcoulakis, Terpsihori was apprehensive about the marriage contract and what would be in store for her in the future. However, she accepted the fact that she would marry the Greek from America, whom she believed to be a wealthy man.

Terpsihori was a beautiful young woman at twenty-one years of age. She was slender, five feet six, with black hair, big striking brown eyes, and she was going to make a beautiful bride. There was a short courtship before the marriage when George and Terpsihori spent some time together getting acquainted. As short as the courtship was, it was a romantic interlude where they asked each other many questions. They took long walks as they talked, trying to find out as much as they could about each other. George spoke of a vision he had, with her at his side, raising a family in America. While sitting on a large rock near the water's edge of the Aegean Sea, with a backdrop of the mountains and blue skies, George held Terpsihori's hand, asked her to be his bride, and promised her he would love her and take care of her. Looking into each other's eyes, they saw love in the making and knew it was for a lifetime. This was the first time they kissed. Many years later, George was asked by his son, Michael, if he would have held the Galanis family to the marriage agreement if Terpsihori had told him she could not love him and didn't want to marry him. He said he would not; he would have honored her decision.

Terpsihori was a gorgeous bride, and she and George had a beautiful wedding. They were married on June 29, 1929, in the Greek Orthodox Church on the island of Crete. The wedding ceremony was traditional, with an ancient and meaningful service that has been celebrated for centuries. The service is abundant with symbols that reflect marriage: love, mutual respect, equality and sacrifice. The ceremony consists of two distinct parts, the Betrothal and the Sacrament of Marriage. Everything has a special meaning and significance, including petitions, the crowning, readings from the Bible, the offering of the common cup, the circling of the ceremonial table, and the benediction. At the conclusion of the prayers, the priest joins the hands of the bride and the groom. Their hands are kept joined until the end of the service to symbolize the union and the oneness of the couple.

The wedding reception lasted for several days, as it was not unusual for wedding celebrations to last a week or longer. There were ample foods and beverages. Everyone thoroughly enjoyed it. Many toasts were made, wishing George and Terpsihori happiness in their marriage, and many offerings were given for a wonderful and happy future in America.

# CHAPTER 2:

# *Their Ocean Voyage to America - A Challenging New Life*

After a short honeymoon, they left for the United States. Their trip was on board a luxurious ocean liner. On the ship, their honeymoon continued for another ten days, the time it took to cross the Atlantic Ocean. They enjoyed themselves as there was music, dancing, wine, and champagne. Terpsihori was astonished at the amount of food that was served.

There were many Greeks on board ship, making the trip to the United States. Many of them, like George and Terpsihori, were going to start new lives; others were going to visit friends and relatives. The ten-day trip was an experience they would never forget. George would remark that his first trip in 1912 was on the British ocean liner *Lusitania* and took nineteen days to cross the Atlantic. Three years later, in 1915, the *Lusitania* would be torpedoed and sunk by a German submarine, killing hundreds of civilians, including many American citizens. This incident and the sinking of other American ships in the Atlantic were factors that caused the United States to enter World War I.

The ocean trip was coming to an end. They entered the United States through Ellis Island in New York. Standing at the rail of the ship, Terpsihori was awed at her first sight of the United States and astonished at the beauty of her new country as they entered New York Harbor. The Statue of Liberty somehow assured her that everything was going to be all right in her new country. She was excited, but her apprehension remained and...yes, she was scared.

They traveled by bus and train across the United States to Sunnyside, Utah. Sunnyside was just the first of several coal-mining towns in which she would live. She soon learned that her life was not to be of leisure and luxury, as she had thought it would be. She was devastated, disappointed, and cried a lot.

Keep in mind, the year was 1929, and there were few conveniences and luxuries available in coal-mining towns. George was a very loving husband and knew that their beginning together under these circumstances was going to be difficult for his wife. He tried to assure her that everything would be all right.

Terpsihori's thoughts were of her home in Greece where she could look out on the beautiful Aegean Sea and, depending on the time of day, see the changing colors of the water with elegant greens and blues. The water was so clear that one could see the rocky bottom and fish swimming thirty feet below the surface. In the early mornings the water would appear to be an emerald green and, as the day progressed into sunset and evening, the colors would become different shades of blue. She thought she would never see this beautiful harbor or the Aegean Sea again.

She left a life of comfort and the protection of her mother and father. Not to be able to see or talk to her sisters or brother was unimaginable. She left her beautiful Greece and family to take on a new life in the Rocky Mountains, which she saw as a barren, forsaken land. Why would anyone want to live in such a place?

It didn't take her long to make friends because there were many other Greek women in the exact same situation. The women depended on each other and would help each other if the occasion called for it.

Many of the Greek coal miners who migrated to the United States were single. This was true of George when he first came to America in 1912 with many other Greeks who were recruited to work the coal mines. A big recruitment drive was made to hire as many Greeks as they could because the word was that the Greeks were excellent workers.

Advertisements showing former Greeks, "labor agents in America," appeared in all the newspapers on the Greek main-land and in Crete. Steamship agents traveled from coastal towns to steep mountain villages and amazed their coffeehouse audi-ences with exaggerated stories of easy money in America. "Work is everywhere. Your two hands are all you need."

The economy of Greece had become unsteady. The pov-erty of the country became one of acute suffering. For many Greeks there was only one hope, America. George had a cousin, who was a miner in Utah, who had already written and told him about the opportunities in the United States. George accepted the offer to become a coal miner. He believed that by going to the new world he would make his fortune. Indeed, many were making their fortunes but, as the years went by, one important part of their lives was missing - having a Greek wife and fam-ily. There were only a few Greek women in Carbon County and they were married. George wanted a wife, preferably a Greek woman from the old country.

In the early 1920s, the American Hellenic Educational Progressive Association (AHEPA), an international fraternal asso-ciation, was created in the United States with chapters in Canada, Australia, the Bahamas, and Greece. Membership includes American citizens of Hellenic descent. Most of the Greeks who came to the United States, and became American citizens, joined AHEPA. One of the main objectives of AHEPA was to promote and encourage patriotism among its members to their adopted country and to instill in them an appreciation of the privileges of citizenship.

In 1929 AHEPA organized a trip to Greece primarily for Greek men who were looking for brides to bring back to the

United States so they could start raising a family. Many Greek men took the opportunity of this trip to do just that. George, who was a proud member of AHEPA, was one of several men from Carbon County to take advantage of this trip.

Through George's family, a marriage contract was drawn up between the Marcoulakis and Galanis families. George sent five dollars to seal the contract. Along with the five dollars, George sent a photograph of himself dressed up in a new suit and seated in a 1929 brand-new Studebaker. George was indeed a very handsome man, and Terpsihori fell in love with a photograph of the man who would soon be her husband.

George had done very well for himself from 1912 to 1929, the year he went back to Greece to get married. George was making a name for himself. He was highly respected and well thought of throughout the coal-mining industry. He could bring out more coal than any other miner. He was prospering and doing very well. He had purchased several automobiles, opened a bakery, and was making good money.

Even with this, times were still pretty hard for Terpsihori, as she had been a spoiled young lady in Greece. Her family was considered upper class and was financially well off. Terpsihori had very few chores, if any, in Greece; her parents had hired help who did all the household chores. She finished high school and was on her way to becoming a school teacher.

*Terpsihori's Mother and Father: Michael and Katherine Galanis*

*Galanis Family: Maria – Katherine – Olympia – Michael – Nick*

*George's Mother and Father: John and Rose Marcoulakis*

*Marcoulakis Family: Eleni – Maria – Rose – John – Cligea*

*George in his 1929 Studebaker. Picture sent to Greece as part of the contractual marriage.*

*George courting Terpsihori on the Island Of Crete, Greece June 1929.*

*Courting Terpsihori in 1929*

*George and Terpsihori Wedding Picture: June 29, 1929, Crete, Greece*

*Terpersihori, Priest and her Mother on her Wedding day on June 29, 1929, Crete, Greece*

*George & Terpsihori with burro on honeymoon, Crete, Greece, 1929. (Cover)*

# CHAPTER 3:

# *The Depression Years*

The year was now 1930, the Depression had hit, and work was not as plentiful as it had been. Terpsihori's first child, a son, was born on March 29, 1930, in the small coal-mining town of Sunnyside, Utah. He was named John, after George's father.

Greek custom decrees that the child be given the father's first name for his middle name. Thus the new baby was named John George Marcoulakis. With the tradition going back for generations, George's middle name was John, as he took his father's first name as his middle name. Even the girls were given their father's first name as their middle name. So, Terpsihori took her father's first name and was named Terpsihori Michael Galanis. This tradition has existed with Greek families for hundreds of years.

When John was a few months old, he contracted a viral infection. His body temperature rose dangerously high. Terpsihori became very distraught over the illness and the thought of losing her precious baby. The Greek doctor who came to the house diagnosed John as gravely ill and told his parents that the baby probably would not survive the night. John had yet to be baptized and Terpsihori and George asked the doctor to baptize the baby before he left. In a tub of very warm water, the doctor submerged John and baptized him according to the baptismal rituals of the Greek Orthodox Church. The submersion of the baby in the warm water caused a badly infected abscess in his ear to drain. Within the hour his fever broke and John immediately started getting better. Terpsihori gave thanks for what she, George, and others believed to be a miracle.

As the Depression continued, things got harder. George moved his family to some of the other coal-mining towns where there was work. They managed, but times were still difficult.

Terpsihori was again pregnant and, on October 18, 1931, she gave birth to her second son. He was named Michael, after her father. Michael George was born in Mutual, Utah. In those days no one in Mutual braved the deep snowdrifts in the winter for a trip to the hospital. Michael was delivered by a midwife.

In September 1985, fifty-four years later, Mike had the opportunity to meet his now ninety-five-year-old midwife, Clara Mangus, at the Greek Carbon County Reunion. She told Mike and his brothers that she remembered delivering Mike like it was yesterday. It had been snowing constantly, the snowdrifts were high and no one could drive in that heavy snow. She stated that she delivered Mike on one day, then delivered another baby the next day who was also named Mike - a Mike Mavarakis. The Mavarakis family and the Markulises are cousins on George's side of the family. Today, Mutual is one of many ghost towns in Utah.

Back in 1931, Terpsihori must have felt overwhelmed and despondent. The house was an old shack with no running water or electricity. She had to wash clothes in a small stream near the house. The first day she walked down to the stream to do the wash she saw a big cat walking toward her. Speaking in Greek and making hand gestures, she tried to shoo the cat away. It was then that a neighbor saw what was going on and chased the cat away. The neighbor explained to Terpsihori that the big cat was a mountain lion that had come down to the stream to drink water. He told her that mountain lions are dangerous and will kill a human being if they are hungry enough. Terpsihori got upset over the thought of dangerous animals in the mountains. She now had to worry about mountain lions with a newborn baby and John, who was then eighteen months old.

Terpsihori wondered if things would ever get better. The depression was taking its toll on her and her family. Even though there was very little work and very little income, she was able to manage.

They then moved to Helper, another small Utah coal-mining town, about two blocks long. The town got its name from the little locomotives called "helpers" that helped push the trains loaded with coal up the mountains. The population was approximately twelve hundred people.

Terpsihori now had a house with running water and electricity. There was even a bathroom in the house. In the winter, temperatures could drop to twenty degrees at night. Using the outhouse with snow and ice on the ground made for a quick trip to the toilet. No more outhouses! Helper was like being in heaven to her. It was a metropolis compared to the other coal-mining towns.

It was in Helper that she gave birth to her third son. He was born on December 18, 1933, and named Nicholas George, after her brother. She was disappointed, because she had wanted a little girl.

With three sons - John was now three years old, Mike was two, and the newborn – Terpsihori was constantly on the go. John and Mike were a handful, as they both were going through their terrible twos! It was a wonder that Terpsihori didn't have a nervous breakdown.

George was of little help to her, as his long working hours kept him in the mines. A coal miner's life was not an easy one, and Terpsihori learned to understand the hardship he had to endure in order to support his family. She also appreciated the dangers involved in being a coal miner and prayed each day when he left for the mines that no harm would come to him or any of the other miners. When he came home in the late evening, she would give thanks for his safe return. At night she would always light her little candles beneath the icons of the Virgin Mother and Jesus Christ, pray and give thanks for all the things she had and for her family in Greece.

Terpsihori, as well as all the other wives and children, knew that accidents in the coal mines were frequent. When a coal-mining disaster occurred, whether it was an industrial accident or a cave-in, it was inevitable that there would be serious injuries and the possibility of the loss of life.

One of the most remembered and talked about mining disasters occurred in the mines of Castle Gate on March 8, 1924. A mine explosion killed 172 men, leaving 417 dependents. George was working on that day but not in the mines of Castle Gate. Many of George's dear friends were killed or injured in that disaster. Almost ten years later, in October of 1933, a good friend and fellow Cretan, Emanuel (Stavrakais) Stavros, died as a result of a mining accident in Kenilworth, Utah. Terpsihori and George were in deep sorrow for the loss of their friend and for his family. The Stavros family remained good friends throughout the many years that followed.

George was injured several times in mining accidents. One serious accident caused him to be hospitalized where he almost lost his right leg. A coal-mining cart, moving on rails, caught George, knocked him to the ground, and broke and mangled his leg. He would never fully recover from this accident. It left him with a noticeable limp, and his leg was shortened about two inches.

When George returned home from the mines, Terpsihori would help prepare her husband's bath by heating water on the stove. She would pour the hot water in a round metal tub and add cold water to it so that the water would be comfortable. There were no bathtubs in most of the homes at that time. The metal tub would be kept outside until there was a need for it, either to bathe or for clothes to be washed. George would come home covered with black coal dust, and the hot bath not only cleansed his body but exhilarated his soul.

Terpsihori always had a warm meal for him, and for the short time that he would stay up in the evening, he enjoyed his family. George was a hard worker, a good husband, and a loving father.

# CHAPTER 4:

# *Sundays and Times of Relaxation*

Coal miners very seldom worked on Sundays. This was the day that the family would relax together. The day always started by going to the Greek Orthodox Church in the town of Price, which was about six miles from Helper—the only Greek Orthodox church for many miles around. Assumption of the Virgin Mary Greek Orthodox Church was built in 1916. It was the thirty-third Greek Orthodox Church in the nation and still is Utah's oldest Greek church in continuous use.

All the Greeks from the other mining towns would assemble at the church for services and other community functions. There were many potluck dinners and even an occasional picnic.

Terpsihori always looked forward to Sundays. The women would enjoy each other's company and discuss the latest happenings. They would exchange recipes and talk about the various types of Greek food. Terpsihori learned to cook from these women, because she had done very little cooking in Greece. Over time, her cooking became second to none, and all raved about her delicious meals.

Children would also have a good time when they were brought together at Greek functions. They would be found playing cowboys and Indians, baseball, football, or whatever sport happened to be in season. One of their favorite pastimes was riding the billy goats, when they were available. When the children got on their backs, the goats would start bucking like wild horses or bulls at a rodeo.

Terpsihori always warned John and Mike not to let the big boys encourage them to ride the goats. It was usually the smaller boys who would ride. The bigger boys loved to watch John ride.

He was about four years old at the time, was a terror at this age, and was easily talked into doing these types of things. He could stay on a bucking goat for quite a long time before getting thrown off. Several times, when he was thrown off, he landed on his head, getting cuts and bruises. He couldn't help boasting how he got the scars. Terpsihori would get infuriated and spank John at the same time as she was cleansing and dressing the lacerations. As they were growing up, both John and Mike acquired battle scars - John a few more than Mike.

Terpsihori never knew from one day to the next what trouble her two little boys would get into. Although George was very caring, it was Terpsihori who had to deal with the day-to-day problems with the boys. George would just tell John and Mike to be careful when riding the goats. He knew that the boys were having fun and that John, who was liked by all, loved riding the goats. Mike idolized his older brother and followed him everywhere. Whenever they got into trouble, it would usually be John who got scolded.

The menfolk would entertain themselves by playing cards. It was not unusual for some of the men to bring their mandolins and violins. They would play and sing Greek songs, reminiscing about their Greek heritage and culture. Other activities included picnics and Greek dances held in the basement of the church. Not to be forgotten were the many weddings and baptisms that took place. The parties that followed these events were classic. Each of the families involved tried to have a bigger and better celebration than any other.

Another outlet for the Greek men was going to the Greek coffeehouses, or *kafeneios*. There were always one or two of these coffeehouses in towns where Greek families lived. Coffee and soft drinks were sold. The Greek/Turkish coffee was so thick that you could cut it with a knife. There was an art in making it, and it had to be thick and sweet.

George frequented the coffeehouse in Helper, and Terpsihori didn't object. She knew it was relaxing for him, especially after a hard day's work in the mine. She had also learned to brew the coffee to perfection, which brought joy to her husband when she made it for him. Women were not allowed to go into these establishments; it was considered unseemly. Small-time gambling also often took place, with men playing cards and dominoes. It seemed that the Greek miners appreciated and respected each other's hard work, knowing that their hard-earned money was needed to support their families. They would sneak some liquor in occasionally, mainly a Greek liquor called *ouzo*. Utah is a dry state and regulates liquor sales, so ouzo was illegal. If the drinkers were caught, there would be a very stiff fine.

CHAPTER 5:

# *Moving to Pennsylvania*

The next few years continued to be difficult, as the Depression had not eased up; in fact, it had gotten worse. There wasn't enough work in the coal mines. Employment was scarce for everyone. George received a letter from a friend who owned a lumberyard in Pennsylvania, and he offered George a job if he would move there. George decided to take him up on the offer.

The year was 1935 and George had made the decision to move his family to Pennsylvania. The move was very disturbing to Terpsihori, and she knew it was going to be an enormous undertaking. She could not take her furniture and other personal possessions that she had gradually been able to acquire. She would have to sell them or give them away. Her biggest concern was her three small children. John was now five, Michael was four, and Nicholas was two. How was she going to manage such a long journey with three small children and very little money? But her deep religious faith made her feel that everything would work out.

George owned a 1929 Studebaker that started with a crank. To start it, one would have to set the spark, which was located on the steering wheel, and then turn the crank, which would start the motor. Fortunately, it was a big car, and it was in this car that the journey was to be made. What belongings could be loaded in the car, on the roof, on the running boards and on the back of the car were loaded and tied down. There was barely enough room inside for the family.

Final arrangements were made. Terpsihori and George said their good-byes to their close and wonderful friends. They started their long journey east on an early morning in the month of

September. The three boys didn't quite understand, other than they were going on a long ride, but they were excited about it.

The trip took two slow and tedious weeks. The family traveled by day, stopping to use restrooms and wash up, and slept in the car at night. Most of the meals were sandwiches with milk or water. Although the weather was good for most of the trip, on several occasions there were storms with torrential rains that flooded the roads. The old Studebaker would sometimes be in water up past the running boards, and the car would stall. All, except Nicholas, would have to get out and push. Most people were sympathetic when they saw a man, a woman, and two small boys pushing a car. They offered to push or tow the car to higher ground, and many of them gave food to help out. It was amazing how people helped one another during the Depression years. All felt the crunch, one way or another, and they would help a fellow human being when one was in dire need.

Everyone in the family was exhausted from the long journey and grateful when it came to an end. The destination was Burgestown, Pennsylvania. Although it was a small colonial town, it was much larger than the coal-mining towns in Carbon County, Utah. George's friend, Costas Pinochis, helped George and Terpsihori get settled. With his help, they were able to find a small two-bedroom house. Mr. Pinochis even helped with the first month's rent.

Mr. Pinochis was the owner of the lumberyard that George was supposed to work in, but George and Terpsihori soon learned that by the time they arrived, there were no jobs available. Upon hearing this, both George and Terpsihori became despondent and felt the trip was to no avail. This long journey left them no better off than they were in Utah. They both were beside themselves and saddened by the circumstances they now found themselves in. They were worried and concerned about how they were going to make a living, and how they would provide for the welfare of their three sons. What was in store for them? What was going to happen to the family?

After the family had settled down, with the help of the local Greek church and Greek families in the community, things began to look a little brighter. Their new friends helped provide supplies and some furniture.

There was coal mining in the region, and that was one thing that George knew he could do and excel at. Terpsihori started taking in washing and ironing to help out. Finding berries and other fruit abundant at that time of year in Pennsylvania, she also learned to can fruit. She learned well, and before long she began to sell jars of preserves and jams. She also learned to can tomatoes and other fruits and vegetables. John and Mike also helped their mother with the canning. They would wash the jars and help mix the ingredients in large kettles while the fruit mixture was cooking.

She would take her three sons with her to pick berries in the fields. John and Mike learned how to pick the berries so they could help their mother. Terpsihori would get a kick out of watching her sons, because they would eat almost as much as they picked. Berry-picking day turned out to be a day they all looked forward to enjoying.

As always, Terpsihori quickly made many new friends, and they helped each other out, especially if a family was in need. She had a wonderful ability to reach out no matter where she would go. Living in a Greek community made it easy for one family to help another. Most families spoke very little English, so communication was always a problem. The men seemed to learn to speak English faster than the women because their jobs required them to converse in English. Both George and Terpsihori said that the Greeks in Pennsylvania and the eastern part of the United States seemed to be friendlier than the Greeks in the Midwest and West.

Soon, George was working again in the coal mines, and the family was doing all right, but the coal-mining industry in Pennsylvania was not much better than coal mining back in Utah. George and Terpsihori missed their old friends and hoped that someday they would go back to Utah.

# CHAPTER 6:

# *Wintertime and a New Baby*

During the winter of 1936, the family discovered that winters in Pennsylvania were much more severe than those in Utah. The temperature was a lot colder, and there was much more snow and ice than in Utah. But the cold weather, ice, and snow did not keep John or Mike from playing outdoors. They never knew when to quit and go inside. On one occasion, Mike ran into the house crying something terrible. He was wearing cotton gloves, and they were soaking wet, his hands freezing cold. His mother took off his gloves and saw that his hands were suffering from frostbite. She took Mike outdoors, packed his hands with snow, and then rubbed his hands together with the snow until they thawed out. She kept massaging until there was some feeling and sensation back in his hands. As a result of the frostbite, Mike's hands would ache whenever he found himself in very cold weather. Gloves wouldn't help after temperatures dropped to freezing.

Although there were many moments that Terpsihori would have loved to strangle the daylights out of her rambunctious sons, she was always a caring and loving mother to all of them. When Terpsihori found herself pregnant again, she was somewhat apprehensive about having another baby at a time when they were struggling to make ends meet. Throughout her nine months of pregnancy, she continued to take in washing and ironing and continued canning fruits and vegetables. She never skipped doing her chores.

On January 30, 1937, Terpsihori gave birth to her fourth son, Costas George Markulis. He was named after their family friend, Costas Pinochis, who would later also baptize the baby.

Again she was disappointed, as she had prayed for a little girl. It was just not meant to be. George, on the other hand, was in his glory because he now had four sons to carry on the Markulis name. George, being the only male child in his family, could rest assured that the Markulis name would live on. George bought a box of cigars, which he passed out to all his friends. The baptismal party lasted for several days, with plenty of good food to eat and liquor to drink. George thoroughly enjoyed himself, as he and Terpsihori were the envy of many people. The four boys were his pride and joy. This was the only time the boys ever saw their father have a little too much to drink!

For some reason, Costas was soon being called "Charles," and eventually, everyone called him Chuck. None of the brothers, not even Chuck himself, could ever recall how or why his name was changed. His mother and father would call him "Chiacos," which was their way of saying Charles in Greek.

George heard that the mines around Canonsburg, Pennsylvania, were paying better than the mines he was working in at the time, and he decided to move his family to that small town. George was such a skillful miner that if there was work to be had, he never had any difficulty getting a job. In a short time, George got a job and had steady employment. All seemed to be going well for the family. George even traded in his 1929 Studebaker for a new 1936 Ford. It was modern, blue in color, and a classy car compared to the Studebaker.

Terpsihori was concerned about the purchase of the new car because it meant that the payment for the car would be taken from the household expenses, but she also knew that the old Studebaker was costing too much for repairs. George was happy and pleased with the purchase of the Ford. It gave him a sense of accomplishment and being successful. In truth, the bottom line was that he simply liked cars. The boys also enjoyed the car, and it was hard keeping them out of it. They would pretend to be driving it and going on a trip.

When his father brought the car home, Mike immediately ran out of the house and got in the new car. Unfortunately, he had the measles and was supposed to stay inside his already quarantined house. Measles are contagious, and vaccines were not available at the time. The doctor or the health department would post a sign on the front of a house to warn others that someone in that household had a communicable disease, and the house was under quarantine. It didn't take long before the rest of the boys came down with the measles.

John was now seven years old, Mike was six, Nick was four, and Chuck was still in diapers. John and Mike were ready to start school. There were no preschool or kindergarten classes at the time, so John and Mike started school together. The year before, John had taken ill and was bedridden. He had somehow contracted a form of blood disease. Because of his illness, John was unable to start school until the following year. So, he and Mike were first-grade buddies together. To hear John talk about the illness, he would tell you that he had poisoned his system from eating too much candy, and that he gorged himself with a Greek candy called *halva*.

Because she was so concerned about him, Terpsihori attended to him day and night. She didn't realize that with all this love and care, she was spoiling him; he was the one getting all the attention. On one occasion, John had been given a toy, and he wouldn't let anyone else play with it. Mike kept trying to take the toy away from him, but John would resist giving it up and would raise a fuss. Terpsihori was constantly threatening Mike and telling him to leave his brother alone, but Mike was not about to give up. One day, while trying to take the toy away, he hit John on the nose with one of his mother's shoes, and the blow caused John's nose to bleed. Terpsihori was furious at Mike, because she had a difficult time stopping the nosebleed, and the bleeding lasted a long time.

It wasn't long after that incident that Mike hit John again on the nose and, again, it caused another nosebleed. As a result of the loss of blood, John became very anemic. To hear John tell this part of the story, these nose bleeds got rid of the diseased blood from his system. John would tell you that his brother Mike saved his life.

Terpsihori went through some difficult times with her sons, especially John and Mike, trying to keep them out of mischief. She never knew from one day to the next what they were going to get into.

When school started, John and Mike were in the same first-grade classroom together. Terpsihori thought that once the boys were in school that they would settle down. Mike settled down a little, but John was still a little terror. On one occasion, John did something to provoke the teacher. In those days the teacher carried a ruler in her hand and would swat a kid or smack the kid on the back of the hand when the child misbehaved.

She walked up to John to give him a couple of smacks with the ruler. The rulers and yardsticks were pretty thick, and when you got smacked with one, it hurt. Well, John wasn't about to let the teacher smack him with the ruler, so he took off running, with the teacher chasing him around the classroom and up and down the aisles. When she got close to him, she would swing the ruler and hit him. John finally stopped, got a good grip on the ruler, and pulled it away from the teacher. She tried to take the ruler back, but John was now one mad little boy, and with all the defiance he could muster, he broke the ruler in half.

The teacher went into a tirade and sent John home. George and Terpsihori were also upset with John's behavior and punished him.

CHAPTER 7:

# George Goes Back to Helper

As time went on, George and Terpsihori found that they were not really happy living in Pennsylvania. George's employment slowed down once again, bills were not being paid, and the car was repossessed. George decided he would go back to Utah and send for the family when he got a job and got back on his feet again. This was very difficult for him, because he did not have enough money to move the whole family at one time. Terpsihori was heartbroken, and she knew that times were going to be difficult for her and her sons. Fortunately, George and Terpsihori had cultivated many new friends in the Greek communities of Pennsylvania. She knew she could rely on them, and they would be there for her if she needed them.

George left by bus for the journey back to Helper. One can only imagine the pain that both he and his wife were feeling, because this was their first separation since they were married. It was a difficult decision, but one they both felt had to be made.

Terpsihori and her four boys moved into a small apartment. The apartment belonged to a little old man who had had one leg amputated. He allowed Terpsihori and her sons to live in the apartment free on the condition that she would clean his house and allow him to have his meals with the family. She had to go on welfare, and she again started taking in washing and ironing to help make ends meet.

With George gone, disciplining the boys became the responsibility of Terpsihori alone. With her two rambunctious sons, John and Mike, always getting into trouble, heaven only knows how she survived! But she was a remarkable woman, and her love for her children was unconditional. She would pray for them and her husband, believing that everything would work out, and that she and her boys would soon join her husband in Utah.

Terpsihori was a very religious woman, and her faith in God helped her maintain her sanity. Every evening she would go through her little prayer ritual of lighting small candles beneath her icons. The icons were very old, having been passed down from generation to generation within her family. They were some of her prized possessions, and they meant the world to her. After her death, the icons were passed on to her sons and grandchildren.

During those Depression years, the streets of Canonsburg became playgrounds, and it was not unusual for children to stay out late at night. John and Mike were no exception. They played until dark, which caused Terpsihori to worry a lot. She would threaten them and tell them she would call the police and have them taken away. Actually, all the kids knew the officer who walked the neighborhood beat and gave him a hard time. He also knew all the children. The kids would call him "bow-legged bananas" because his legs were bowed. The kids would pull pranks on him in the dark, then run and hide. He actually took a liking to the children, and as long as they were not doing anything criminal, he would go along with the pranks.

During the summer months when school was not in session, John, Mike, and some of their friends would walk several miles to a large pond to go fishing. Fishing poles were made of long sticks or thin tree branches, regular string, and a safety pin tied on the end of the string for a fish hook. To get to the pond, they would follow the railroad tracks. There were different kinds of fish in the pond, particularly catfish. The poles with the safety pins got plenty of nibbles, but no fish.

The pond was surrounded with trees, tall grass, and lots of brush; it was an ideal place for kids to play, as long as they didn't go swimming. The pond wasn't very deep, and the bottom was all quicksand. If you got caught in it, you could easily get stuck. If someone else wasn't close by or didn't have a branch, pole, or some other means to help, you could easily get sucked down into the quicksand.

On one of their excursions to the pond, the boys built a raft with items found around the pond area. When it was finished, they pushed it into the water. John and Mike got on the raft and tried to push the raft out into the pond with poles. The raft immediately began to take on water and started to sink. John and Mike both jumped off and watched it as it sank.

Although this incident was never told to their mother, Terpsihori somehow learned about their trips to the pond and how dangerous it was because of the quicksand. She repeatedly warned the boys not to go to the pond, for it was a dangerous place, especially for children. Finally, the town posted warning signs at locations around the pond, warning people of the quicksand.

Sometimes John and Mike left the pond after it was dark. There were no lights, and the darkness made it difficult to see. On clear nights, the sky would reveal millions of stars. Adding to the magnificent glitter of the stars were the fireflies that lit up the night. John and Mike would catch as many as they could and put them in a glass jar. Flying around inside the jar, the fireflies would turn the jar into a lantern. By its light, the boys followed the railroad tracks that led them back to their house.

One night, when John and Mike got home, they knew their mother was angry. They looked through the living room window and saw her talking to the police officer who walked the neighborhood beat. In her broken English, she was trying to tell the officer that her boys had not come home. Not only was she furious, but she also was worried. She wanted the officer to put a scare into her sons, hoping that it might change their behavior.

After the officer left, John and Mike got up enough courage to go into the house, and they got one of the worst scoldings they had ever had. Terpsihori yelled and screamed at her two sons. During the scolding, she cursed her husband because he had left her with all the responsibility of taking care of the household and children. John and Mike promised that they would behave and not go to the pond anymore. They kept that promise.

There were times when Terpsihori would be alone and lonely. The boys would catch her talking to herself. It would appear as if she were talking to her husband, asking him to hurry and send for them. As the months passed, Terpsihori became stronger, and her sons became more helpful and responsive to her needs.

John and Mike were doing well in school, which was a big relief to her. Though they had settled down, there were still moments when they would do something that would cause her to get upset.

Terpsihori collected nice dishes and china. All her dishes and china were kept in a cabinet. The cabinet stood about seven feet high and had several drawers on the bottom where she kept her linens. One day she hid some candy on one of the shelves, high enough where the boys could not reach it. Mike knew where the candy was, and he knew that by pulling out one of the bottom drawers and standing on it, he would be able to reach the candy. Mike waited till he was the only one in the room. He then pulled out one of the drawers, opened the glass doors, and stood on top of the drawer. As he reached for the candy, his weight on the drawer caused the entire cabinet to fall on top of him. The china and dishes fell out, most of them breaking when they hit the floor.

Terpsihori heard the loud crash and came running into the room. She saw Mike under the cabinet with broken glass all around him, and she panicked. Her first thought was that her son was seriously hurt. Other than hurt pride and the painful prospect of getting a good whipping, Mike had suffered only a few abrasions and scratches. Nevertheless, by pretending to be hurt, he avoided a spanking. Terpsihori was upset at the thought of so many of her nice dishes being broken, especially since it had taken her many years to collect them. At the same time, she was very concerned about Mike and relieved that he wasn't seriously hurt.

Despite the hardships, there were many pleasant times. Terpsihori always managed to take her sons to visit family friends, and she would warn them to be on their best behavior. Any serious misbehavior would result in a firm pinch or a stern look from her. Her pinches were painful, but she only used them when she didn't want to make a scene or make the discipline obvious.

She would always make a delicious dessert to take with her. Most of the time she baked *koulourakia,* a very tasty Greek cookie. They were easy to make and could be taken anywhere without drying out or becoming stale. When she really wanted to make something good, she would bake *baklava.* This was a honey-walnut pastry with many paper-thin layers of *phyllo* dough, both on top and bottom of the pastry. It was topped off with a sweet syrup. She always received compliments on her baklava, and it was one of her sons' favorite desserts as well.

Over the years, Terpsihori learned how to cook, and she always managed to have a delicious meal on the table, followed by dessert. Her rice pudding was delicious, inexpensive to make, and easily prepared. Another inexpensive special treat that she made was her graham crackers and pudding desert. She would stir up a batch of pudding, place graham crackers on the bottom of a deep pan, and then pour the pudding over the crackers. She would have several layers of crackers and pudding. It would then be cut in squares and served. All four of her sons were never disappointed and always looked forward to her wonderful meals and desserts.

You will recall that Terpsihori, as a young lady in Greece, did not cook or bake. Her family, being well off, had hired help to do it. When leaving as a new bride for America, her mother made sure she packed a cookbook to take with her to the United States. With the aid of the cookbook, help from her women friends in the Greek community, and her own intuitive and creative ideas, she became an outstanding cook. Complimented on her tasty meals, she took pride in sharing her recipes with others, but she had no precise measurements. It was always a pinch of this, a small handful of that, and so on. Never was there a true measurement. It was her own feel of the texture and taste of the ingredients that made her meals and pastry dishes delicious.

Her husband, George, was also an excellent cook and baker. They were always competing with each other about who was the better cook. This was especially true many years later when George retired, and the two of them would cook or bake something special for their children, grandchildren, and great-grandchildren. They would both be playfully critical of each other's cooking. It was comical to watch the two of them trying to get their children to side with them. Actually, they were both excellent cooks.

All these years later, they are thought of constantly and missed so very much, especially around the holidays.

CHAPTER 8:

# *George Sends For His Family*

Terpsihori's prayers were finally answered when George sent her money for bus fare for the family to return to Utah. Everyone was excited, especially Terpsihori. She was happy about the news and couldn't wait for this Pennsylvania ordeal to come to an end.

Once again Terpsihori would have to pack up those possessions she wanted to take and have them mailed to Helper. Again, she had to sell or give away many items. She had gone through this before and knew she would be able to manage. She gave things to her friends and neighbors who needed them. This gave her an opportunity to thank friends who had been kind to her during those difficult times. Many had been there for her when she needed them. The boys also had made many friends, and now it was time for them to say good-bye. Moving and leaving friends was always difficult, and it seemed that the family had faced this moment far too often.

Terpsihori was worried that the trip back to Helper would take several days and that she would have to closely watch her sons to make sure they didn't wander off or get lost, especially when changing buses or waiting at bus stops. Because her English was very limited, she knew she would have to rely on John and Mike to interpret for her.

The trip was made on a comfortable Greyhound bus, and each member of the family had his own seat. The boys could even get up and walk a little through the aisle. In addition to periodic stops, there were several points when they would need to change buses. For a woman with very limited knowledge of English and four small boys, including an infant, the trip was going to be quite a challenge. But Terpsihori was a determined woman, and she wasn't going to miss any stops or bus changes.

The bus drivers understood her challenges and tried to be considerate. John was a lot of help to his mother, not only by interpreting but also by keeping Mike and Nick under control. John was on his best behavior and really helped his mother during the trip.

Nevertheless, the long bus ride was not exactly a pleasant experience. The boys would get tired and get out of their seats to walk around. They were not used to sitting down for long periods. Everyone on the bus, including Terpsihori and the boys, would look forward to the next bus stop. There was always a small café, and Terpsihori made sure everyone had something to eat. The meals were mainly scrambled eggs, toast, and a glass of milk. Terpsihori had also made a big batch of those Greek koulourakia cookies, which she gave to the boys when they were hungry.

On several occasions, one of the boys got carsick and threw up. No matter how well Terpsihori cleaned up the mess, there remained a foul stench in the bus. There really was nothing else she could do. At the next stop, the bus would be cleaned, aired out, and deodorized.

At last, the bus pulled into the depot in Helper. It was late afternoon, and the sun was on the western horizon. To the east, the mountain range reflected hues of orange and red, and they could see Balance Rock, Helper's well-known landmark.

Looking out the windows, the family could see George waiting for them, and he had a smile on his face; he was excited to see his wife and sons home again. It had been over six months since George had left them to go back to Helper, but it seemed a lot longer to all of them. Terpsihori was very happy and relieved that they were back in Helper and together as a family. There were hugs, kisses, and tears during this reunion. As happy as

Terpsihori was, she couldn't hold back from telling George what a terrible situation he had left her in and what a difficult time she had had trying to make ends meet and keep the boys out of trouble. George tried to explain why it took so long for him to send for them.

While George and Terpsihori were having their discussion, the boys stretched their legs and started running up and down the familiar street. Although they had been gone for three years, the town had not changed. George took his family to a hotel where they were to stay for several days because the house George had rented was not quite ready for them to move into.

To this day, the brothers remember Helper's landmark, Balance Rock, which sits on the north edge of the mountain range and is enormous in size. It gives an illusion that it is balanced, as if it was deliberately placed there, and if anyone would push the rock, it would tumble down the mountain range. On top of the rock stands a pole twenty-five to thirty feet high. In 1929, a group of Helper's citizens climbed the mountain, scaled the huge rock and placed the pole on top of it. A flag was then placed on the top of the pole. As the flag became shredded by the weather, it would be replaced. The last item placed on the pole was a one hundred pound grease drum. Holes were cut for drainage, and the drum was half filled with rocks to hold it down. The drum still remains on the pole today.

Many years later, when Mike was a Los Angeles police officer assigned to work the vice squad, he learned a funny thing about Helper. He was investigating prostitution activity in several hotels in San Pedro, California. The madams who operated these hotels were also the owners of the hotel in Helper where, so long ago, the family had stayed. They were operating prostitutes out of that hotel, catering to the coal miners and railroad workers. Mike also learned that the madams owned hotels in several other states. They would put the women on what they called a "wheel" and move them every two or three months from one hotel to another. The "wheel" kept the women from becoming too comfortable in any one place and, at the same time, they moved on too quickly for the police to really know who they were or where they worked.

# CHAPTER 9:

# *A Struggle, but Good to Be Back Home*

George moved his family into a small two-bedroom house situated at the base of the mountain range where Balance Rock was located. In fact, there was nothing behind the house except large gullies, lots of wildflowers, weeds, and the mountain range. Terpsihori was not too thrilled with the house, especially when she found that the toilet was an outhouse.

She had never thought she would find herself in this situation again! To use the toilet meant that she and the family would have to go outside and walk thirty or forty feet to a five-foot-by-five-foot shed that stood seven feet high. In the shed was a pit toilet with no running water. The waste would accumulate, and once it got to a certain point, a new hole would be dug and the same shed would be placed on top of it. The old hole would then be filled with dirt.

The house was one of three houses that George would move his family into during the next few years. This house, as well as the others, had a character all its own, and each home had its own story.

Their present home, located at the base of the mountain range, made an ideal playground for the boys, at least as long as they were careful. One could find mountain lions, scorpions, lizards, rattlesnakes, and other types of reptiles and animals in the mountains. The rattlesnakes and scorpions were the biggest hazards, because many of the townspeople had been bitten by a rattlesnake or stung by a scorpion. They were both highly venomous, and the person would have to be treated right away. To

Terpsihori's dismay, Mike and John would collect scorpions and play with them, tease them with a small stick, and try to get them to fight each other. Both boys had been stung by scorpions while walking or playing outdoors. The sting was very painful and was treated by placing mud over the sting to draw out the stinger and the venom. The stings were rarely fatal, but the venom could cause you to have a high temperature and feel sick for a few days.

But when comparing the mischief the boys had been getting into in Pennsylvania with what they found to do in the mountainous terrain of Helper, which the boys used as a playground, Terpsihori preferred Helper. She got to the point where she accepted what she had, and she became immune to almost anything as long as she was with her husband and her children. She lived a difficult life during those Depression years, especially raising four boys, but it made her a stronger person. I think she wouldn't have had it any other way. Many years later, Terpsihori said that all the mothers and wives who struggled through that period were remarkable women, and they were the ones who kept their families together.

To make up for the outhouse, George made sure that Terpsihori had a washing machine, which she appreciated because she would no longer need to wash clothes by hand. The washing machine was the kind where you would put the wet clothes through two rollers and the pressure of the rollers would wring the clothes so there was no water left in them. If the clothes got too bunched up or got stuck while going through the rollers, a safety mechanism built into the wringer would release the pressure on the clothes.

On one occasion, Terpsihori wished she didn't have the washing machine. Nick, who was about five years old now, found the washing machine intriguing and put his hand between the two rollers as the machine was running. The rollers grabbed on to his hand and started pulling it through the rollers. He started screaming, and Terpsihori turned around just in time to see Nick's hand and arm being pulled through the ringer. She immediately hit the safety release that took the pressure off of his arm. To her distress and Nick's, the rubber rollers had adhered to Nick's skin and started pulling some of the skin off, causing his hand and arm to bleed. Terpsihori put compresses on the arm and bandaged it up, but Nick was still a very unhappy five-year-old. After that incident, it took some time for Nick to even walk close to the washing machine.

As the washing machine incident proved, Nick was now at the age where he would start getting into mischief. John and Mike were held somewhat responsible for both Nick and Chuck. If the younger boys got into mischief, John or Mike would get scolded or spanked. On one occasion when John and Mike were taking care of Nick, they put him on a homemade swing and began to push him. Nick was yelling, "Higher," and so they pushed him higher. The higher he went, the more he laughed. Then, after one good push, he maxed out on the height, lost his grip on the ropes, fell off the swing, and hit the ground, breaking his arm. He was no longer laughing but crying because of the pain. Terpsihori took Nick to the doctor, who put a cast on his arm. She was furious with John and Mike; after all, they were older and should have known better.

CHAPTER 10:

# Full of Energy and Growing Pains

There were many farmers raising sheep in the area around Helper, along with other farm animals like chickens, goats, a few horses, and even one bison. Two horses belonged to a neighbor, and he allowed John and Mike to ride them occasionally. The one Mike rode was a beautiful chestnut with a white star in the middle of his nose; John rode a gray mare. The boys enjoyed the horses, and their neighbor let them ride as long as they brushed the horses down and fed and watered them.

The boys also helped the farmers herd the sheep from one grazing area to another, which kept John and Mike busy and out of trouble. Mostly, the farmers had dogs that were trained to herd the sheep, and it was fun to watch as they worked and kept the flocks together. If there was more than one dog, the dogs worked as a team, and the farmers never lost any sheep while the dogs were working. The mere presence of the dogs kept the mountain lions away. The sheepherders had a saying that one good sheepdog was better than hiring ten men to work the sheep.

The one bison was enormous. It was dark brown with long, matted hair. The farmer was raising it for slaughter, and he kept it in a pen just large enough for it to move around a little. He would keep the small children from getting too close to it. It wasn't a beautiful animal by any means, but one couldn't get over the size of it and how powerful it looked. The boys had learned about the bison in school and how some of the cowboys of the early west were slaughtering them just for the fun of shooting them. The Indians slaughtered buffalo only for food and used their hides to make clothing. The selfishness of some of the reckless cowboys almost made the buffalo extinct in America.

The sheepherders taught John and Mike how to make slingshots, because they were useful in herding the sheep. After practicing with them for a while, the boys became pretty accurate and could catapult a rock a long distance. They would improve their proficiency by trying to hit cans or other objects. They also took the slingshots with them wherever they would go, especially on the mountain range where they spent most of their leisure time playing.

There were many trails they could follow and ravines to play in. The ravines contained a white crystalline substance called carbide. The boys learned that by putting this substance in a bottle, mixing it with water, and then capping the bottle, the mixture would fizzle, causing pressure to be built up in the bottle. With the pressure built up, they would throw the bottle, and it would cause a small explosion that burned upon impact. On one occasion, John threw one of these bottles on the hillside, and the explosion started the dry brush and grass burning. The fire took off and burned the entire hillside, including part of the cemetery, which was on the top of the hill. The volunteer fire department responded and, with the help of other citizens, put the fire out. No one could figure out what caused the fire, and John and Mike never said anything for fear of getting into trouble. The hillside fire was the talk of the town for several days.

The mountain range also had many streams, and the boys liked to play in the water. Price River was the one main river that flowed through Helper, and it was used to irrigate crops, fruit trees, and alfalfa, which was used to feed the livestock. During the hot summer months, John, Mike, and some of their friends would go swimming in the river. There were several spots where the water was fairly deep, and the boys would dive off the rocks into the river. The river current flowed pretty fast. Ropes were tied across the river so that one could grab on to a rope and not get swept down the river by the current. Most of the time, when the boys went swimming, they would take off their clothes and swim naked. The area had a lot of trees and brush on both sides of the river, and it was unlikely that they would be seen.

Sometimes, after the boys took a swim, they would go on a farmer's property, pick some of the vegetables, wash them, and eat them. Tomatoes, freshly picked, were delicious and a special treat. Cherries, apricots, and peaches were also very good when eaten right after they were picked. If the boys asked the farmers first, they didn't mind. However, most of the time, the boys would not get permission, and the farmers would get angry and chase them away. Occasionally, a farmer would shoot at the boys with a shotgun loaded with rock salt; if someone got hit, the rock salt would cause the skin to sting, and he would end up with a rash. The Price River was also used to keep the town's streets clean through the use of a canal system. The canals were not only used for irrigating crops but also to divert water into the town's gutters. The water running down the gutters kept the streets clean of any litter. For being a coal-mining town, Helper was always a clean town.

A favorite pastime of the children was to make little boats out of wood and race them in the water, either in the river itself or in the canals or gutters. Some of the kids went all out in making some pretty elaborate boats with masts that had strings tied to them. The river always kept clean water running through the canals and gutters.

During the winter months, when it snowed and the temperature got below freezing, water was diverted into a large, shallow man-made pond. The pond was the size of a football field, and it was about three feet deep. The water would freeze and the town's people would use it as an ice skating rink. Terpsihori had purchased several pairs of strap-on ice skates, and the boys would go skating. It was not unusual for them to spend many hours skating on the ice pond.

Signs were posted in certain areas to warn skaters where the ice was too thin to skate on. When the ice was beginning to melt, skaters would occasionally fall through the ice and get all wet. If you kept skating on the pond when it started warming up, it was inevitable that you would eventually fall through the ice; this happened to John and Mike more than once.

During the summer months, the dry pond area was used to play football or baseball. All the boys in town would go down to the pond, sides were picked, and games were played. Tackle football would be played without any pads. The boys played hard from sunrise to sunset. Many baseball games also were played on that dry pond. In fact, in Helper, baseball was the big sport. The adults had a semiprofessional baseball league, and one of the teams was named the Helper Merchants.

The ballplayers on the Helper team took a liking to Nick. He was always at the ball field helping out. He shagged balls and kept the bats lined up. He had become their mascot and batboy. They played their games in a field located adjacent to the town's park. On Sundays when the games were played, families would make a day of it and have a picnic.

The park also had a fairly large swimming pool. John, Mike, and Nick would go swimming there when it was open. The only catch was that it cost a nickel to get in, and there were many times when the boys just didn't have any money. Instead of going in, they would stand on the outside of the enclosed fence and watch everyone swim, or go swimming in the river.

Two dressing rooms were located on opposite sides of the pool, one for the girls and the other for the boys. John and Mike found a way to sneak into the pool without having to pay. There was a small opening for ventilation just below the roof on the back side of the dressing room, which was on the park side. John and Mike would climb up onto the opening and slide into the dressing room. They would change into their swimsuits, carry their clothes outside to the pool area, set them down, and then go swimming.

The boys learned to swim in this pool. They would dive into the deep end from one of the corners and then float under water to the other corner. Some of the bigger boys would pick up John and Mike and throw them into the deep end of the pool, where they had to swim back to the ledge. John got Nick to learn to swim the same way; he would throw Nick out in the deep end and then tell him to swim back.

During some of the holidays, especially the Fourth of July, coins were thrown into the pool. Everyone would dive in, swim to the bottom, and try to get as many coins as they could. The coins varied from silver dollars down to pennies, and both John and Mike always managed to get some of those coins. The big prize, several dollars, went to the person who could catch a swimming fish that was thrown in the water. Many family picnics took place in this park, creating wonderful memories of happy occasions.

# CHAPTER 11:

# *A Bigger and Nicer Home*

Terpsihori felt that the house they were living in was too small, and she told George that she was going to make some inquiries about finding a larger house. After talking to some of her Greek women friends, she found a house that was not too far from where they then lived, and it was next door to the Nickas family, who were Terpsihori's cousins. It was larger, had a good-sized basement, and had a big backyard, with fruit trees and enough room to grow a big vegetable garden. It was the ideal house for the family and especially nice for Terpsihori, since she could live next door to her cousins. The house also had a big front porch where the family could visit with friends when they came over. Terpsihori was excited about the move and looked forward to moving quickly.

George's work at the mine kept him busy working long hours. He would come home tired and sometimes in a bad mood, especially if he had had a bad day at the mine. George was not known to lose his temper very often, but when he did, he would argue with his wife if she had done something that upset him. Terpsihori would get her feelings hurt, but after a short cooling-off period, George would apologize and tell her that he had had a rough day at the mine.

When it came to his sons, George was a strict disciplinarian. The boys knew that they would get into trouble if they didn't mind their mother and do their chores. Usually a stern scolding would suffice, but once in a while a good spanking followed, if warranted.

Mike can still recall the worst spanking he ever got from his father. George had gotten home from the mines late in the day. He was covered from head to foot with black coal dust, and Terpsihori was heating water on the stove for his bath. She needed more coal to put into the stove to heat the water, and she asked Mike to go outside and get some for her. He said he would and went outside to get the coal. He saw his cousin, who lived next door, and they began talking. Mike forgot about the coal.

George was waiting for the coal to heat up the water for his bath. After a short while, he went outside to look for Mike. When he saw Mike talking to his cousin, he became infuriated. He took off his miner's belt, which had to be three to four inches wide, grabbed Mike, and began hitting him with the belt. Mike had never been hit like that before, nor had any of the other boys. Mike hurt from that whipping, but he was more hurt that he had let his father down. All the boys learned from that incident that their responsibilities to their mother and father were paramount. Terpsihori, as usual after such an incident with one of her sons, felt sorry for Mike and soothed his wounds while she talked and comforted him. Many decades later, John told Mike that he had been punished with that same miner's belt.

Terpsihori was no different from most mothers who love their children. She had a special bond with her sons, probably because of the hardships that they had gone through. Having to raise her children during the Depression years, moving from one coal-mining town to another, and trying to save enough money to buy groceries and essentials they needed brought them closer together. Whenever she could do something a little extra or buy something nice for her sons, she did. She had a unique quality about her that made her stand out from many of the other women in the community. She was a giving person, giving of herself not only to her family but also to many of her neighbors and friends. She cherished her sons and would go out of her way for them.

Terpsihori made sure that the boys were dressed warmly during the winter. All year long she would save money for clothes they needed for school. Around the time of the first snowfall, Terpsihori would take her sons to the small general store and buy them boots. The one brand that was popular with all the boys had a small pocket knife enclosed in a holder on the side of one of the boots. The boys were in their glory when they got those new boots.

Winter was a fun time for the boys, as they loved playing in the snow. Terpsihori and George managed to buy one used sled that the boys shared. One time, John came across a sled that had been trashed because one of the runners was broken in half. He learned to ride it by using his strength to keep the broken runner from jamming into the snow. The boys shared the two sleds and would race each other, as well as other friends, down the hills. John and Mike also tried their skill at skiing by taking the staves off a wine barrel and waxing them down. With the staves fastened to their boots, they were able to ski. As silly as it looked, it worked, and the boys had fun trying to stay upright.

Winter was always a beautiful time of the year in Helper. The children enjoyed playing in the snow, making snowmen, and having lots of snowball fights. Some of the boys would put a rock in the center of a snowball and throw it at someone. In fact, it was not unusual for all the boys to do this when they were getting ready to have a snowball fight. Sides would be picked and snowballs made and stockpiled before the fights began. There were some bruises, but no one got seriously hurt. It wasn't unusual to find even the adults occasionally enjoying themselves with the children playing in the snow.

However, the bitter cold was hard on the miners. Working the mines in freezing weather was very uncomfortable. The extra clothing to keep warm restricted their movement, and the cold weather made it harder for them to bring out the coal. This was the time of year when more coal was used to heat up the homes and businesses, and the price of coal was always higher in the winter. Thus families kept their cellars full so they would not run out during the winter months. Terpsihori and the other women found themselves baking more during the winter. The heat from the stoves kept the houses nice and warm. Bread baked in the wintertime always seemed to taste better. Melted butter on a piece of bread right out of the oven was very tasty, as were pastries. With four boys in a household, the pastries didn't last very long.

Another treat that was always popular during the winter months was Jell-O. It was simple to make, but to the boys, it was like a magic ice pudding. Either George or Terpsihori would make it, but mostly, it was George who would mix up a big bowl of Jell-O and then place the bowl on a windowsill on the back porch. After a few hours, the Jell-O was ready to eat. This was a big treat that came only in the cold winter months, as it could not be made during the summer because iceboxes were not cold enough to thicken the Jell-O. No one had refrigerators, and the iceboxes were mainly used to keep milk and food from spoiling.

During the evening hours, the family would sit around the radio and listen to many entertaining programs while eating pastries or Jell-O. Comedy programs, such as *Jack Benny* and *Amos 'n Andy*, were favorites. The family also listened to mystery radio programs, such as *Inner Sanctum*, *The Shadow*, and *The Green Hornet*.

Comic books were also a fun pastime. They were bought for a nickel each, read, and then exchanged or passed on to another brother. After all the boys had read them, they were traded with someone else. It was comical to watch John as he read some of the "funny books," as they were called. He would break out in laughter as he was reading, and sometimes he laughed from the beginning to the very end of the comic book. His laughter was contagious, and before long he had everyone laughing, even though he was the only one reading the funny book. It was fun to watch Terpsihori, as she got a big kick out of John when he went into one of his funny book frenzies, and she would laugh along with him. It was nice to hear her laugh and see her happy. The love she had for her family was obvious and wonderful.

Terpsihori and George were very proud of their sons and worked hard through all the adversities to have a happy home. The close family unity they enjoyed made for a happy home, even with the continuing hard times, because the Depression had not yet ended. Dinnertime was special for the Markulis family, as everyone ate their dinner meal at the same time. George and Terpsihori would talk about what had transpired during the day and anything special that would be coming up. The boys would add to the dinner conversation and talk about what they had done.

George often made toys for the boys out of wood. He was good at making rubber guns and slingshots. Rubber guns were played with a lot. He used a handsaw to shape the gun and then placed a clothespin on the handle by either tying it or securing it with rubber bands. The rubber bands were cut from old inner tubes; once each player had stockpiled a lot of them, the boys would shoot the rubber bands at each other.

CHAPTER 12:

# A Beautiful Red Scooter
# for Christmas

The Christmas season was always a beautiful time of the year. The ground, trees, and rooftops were covered with snow and icicles. Each icicle was of a different length, hanging from the eaves and reflecting a multitude of colors from the rays of the sun or the moon. The cold days and even colder nights made everyone bundle up to stay warm. There was a pleasant feeling about being outdoors at night, looking up into the vast void of darkness, and seeing millions of stars glittering like Christmas lights, dancing in the sky. The nights during these cold winter months seemed to be so much clearer than during the summer. One could almost reach up and touch a star. The nights were beautiful and tranquil. By studying the sky and its beauty, one could find inner peace and closeness to God, the Creator and architect of all of this beauty.

The cold weather didn't stop the young at heart from going outdoors and enjoying the season. It was time for sleigh riding, skiing with the wine-barrel skis, building snowmen or snow fortresses, having snowball fights, or just exploring other ways to enjoy the snow. Children played nonstop, sometimes exhausted by their efforts, and you could see the steam from their breaths in the coldness of the day or night.

What was not fun was having to shovel the snow off the sidewalks and walkways or clear the entrance to one's house. Some winters were worse than others, depending on the amount of snowfall.

On one occasion, Terpsihori told Mike that one of her friends, a woman who lived close by, had accidentally lost two fifty-cent coins in the snow. She asked Mike if he would try to find the coins for her friend. Early the next morning Mike went out with a shovel and got to work. Some of the neighborhood kids wondered what he was doing. When Mike told them that he was looking for some money a family friend had lost, they laughed and said that no one would be able to find any coins in all that snow. After several hours of moving the snow around, Mike found the two fifty-cent pieces. He ran into the house and gave the coins to his mother. Terpsihori took Mike to her friend's house and gave her the coins. She was so grateful that Mike would do that for her that she gave him one of the coins. It was a good deed, graciously rewarded.

On Christmas Eve, before going to bed, each son would hang his stocking by the Christmas tree. George and Terpsihori always managed to put something in each stocking. Upon getting up on Christmas morning, the boys would make a dash for the stockings to see what Santa Claus had left them. There was always a fruit or two, nuts, some hard candy, pennies and nickels, and maybe a dime or two.

Terpsihori and George also seemed to always manage one toy to be shared by all four boys. One Christmas, the toy was a bright red scooter with balloon tires. John probably rode it the most, but the other boys shared it with him. Mike could recall riding this beautiful scooter in the evenings, after the sun went down, and it seemed like he was flying. He could feel the cold air rushing past his face the faster he rode it. The scooter was one of the best gifts the boys ever got, and they knew their mother and father had sacrificed to save for it. Both Terpsihori and George received pleasure from buying the scooter, knowing that their sons enjoyed it so much.

CHAPTER 13:

# Church Activities and Holidays

The Markulis family, like many other families in small towns, always looked forward to church activities and to the different events that took place, both holiday events and community events. Terpsihori made sure that the family went to church on Sundays and participated in most of the church activities. She talked to the priest and signed Mike and John up to be altar boys during church services. Neither John nor Mike wanted any part of it and they resisted, but their mother won out.

The first time Mike served as an altar boy, he was standing close to the priest when he realized he had to go to the bathroom! He was nervous over this ordeal of serving, and that, no doubt, contributed to his predicament. He told the priest several times that he had to go, but the priest kept telling Mike to wait until the services were over. Greek Orthodox services don't last for just one hour; they often last for two hours and sometimes longer. Well, Mike couldn't wait, so he just left and went to the restroom. He returned and resumed his duties during the Mass.

After the Mass, the priest scolded Mike and told him not to ever do that again. Mike told him that he wouldn't, because that was the first and last time he would serve as an altar boy. Of course, that did not make Terpsihori and George very happy. They both tried to convince him to change his mind, but Mike had made his decision, and he was just not going to be an altar boy.

Each member of the congregation would buy a candle and light it during the services. At one point during Easter services, members with the lit candles would walk in a procession around the outside of the church. One Easter, before the procession began, members were sitting in church, including Mike, and he fell asleep holding a lit candle. The candle caught one of the drapes on fire and there was a short panic, but several of the members pulled the drape down and put the fire out. Mike got scared and George and Terpsihori were embarrassed at the thought that one of their sons might have been responsible for burning down the church. As a result of that incident, children were no longer allowed to carry lit candles during those special services.

The cultural holiday known as "name days" is celebrated by all members and families of the Greek Orthodox Church. It honors the saints after which each person is named. Whenever there was a name day and a member of the family was named after that saint, the family would have a party. Greek families often name their sons after saints such as Michael, John, Nicholas, George, Anna, Eva, or any of the many other saints. In order not to hurt anyone's feelings, families would go from one home to another where they were celebrating. There would be no gifts for the person whose name day it was, but people would take food and pastries. Many times if there was food left over from the one party, it would be taken to the next party.

Birthdays were never celebrated, as name days took precedence. However, over the years, the celebration of birthdays also came to be recognized by Greek families.

# CHAPTER 14:

# *1940 - Times Are Good!*

The year was now 1940. John was ten, Mike was nine, Nick was seven, and Chuck was three.

Helper had grown in size, but was still considered a small town. Mike had failed the third grade, not because he was a slow learner or dumb, but because he rebelled against his third-grade teacher. Terpsihori, being from the old country, had not talked to his teacher and did not make any inquiries as to why Mike had failed. In Utah, when you failed a grade, you failed a whole year! (In California at that time, a student who failed a semester, would just need to repeat that one semester, not the full year.)

It was winter, snowing hard, and John, Mike, and Nick walked to school. Because of the slush, the snow, and the long distance they had to walk to get to school, they were a few minutes late one morning. When Mike walked into his classroom, the teacher, Mrs. Knight, punished him for being late. She hit him and embarrassed him in front of his classmates. From that day until the end of the school year, Mike rebelled. He would disrupt the class, not answer any questions, and not turn in any of his homework. On classroom written assignments, he would write crude and ugly remarks on his paper, directed to the teacher. The teacher never sent Mike to the principal's office, and Mike never told his mother or father about the punishment for fear of also being punished by them.

Mike repeated the third grade with a different teacher, and this time he got good grades. His attitude changed and he studied hard. He even won his classroom's spelling bee.

The teacher challenged the students by getting them involved, using various learning techniques. The spelling bee was one technique to get the students interested in reading and spelling. The teacher would have all the students stand up around the classroom and then give one student a word to spell. If the student got the word right, he or she would remain standing. If the word was not spelled correctly, the student would sit down. This exercise continued until there was one student left standing, and that student would then be declared the winner. The teacher would sometimes give the student a prize. After some of the big spelling bees, everyone celebrated with a class party.

On occasion, without the teacher's knowledge, the students would pick a day for a "peanut-bust." The students would buy peanuts in the shell, and then, on a predetermined signal, they would throw the peanuts at the teacher. Her desk would be covered with peanuts. It was done in jest and everyone, including the teacher, would laugh and have a good time. Of course, the real fun came when everyone got to shell and eat the peanuts. Then, after the peanut-bust was over, there was always a mess to clean up.

John and Mike stayed very close together most of the time. When either of them got in a fight after school, the other always stood by and made sure no one else jumped in. If someone did jump in, then the other brother would also get involved in the fight. John and Mike never lost a fist fight and actually established a reputation of being pretty tough. On occasion, during lunch and nutrition breaks, both boys and some of their friends went around the school, challenging anyone to a fight. After a few fights with some upperclassmen, John and Mike were sent to the principal's office. The principal put them on restriction with a stern warning that one more incident would result in their suspension from school.

Even though John and Mike were mischievous, they were excellent students, always getting good grades. In fact, all three sons, including Nick, were good students and they all participated in after-school programs to earn extra credit. The school had a reading program in which prizes and certificates were given to students for reading books. It also put on school plays. As a special treat, John and Mike's class put on a Halloween play for the student body and faculty, and both boys had parts in the play. Terpsihori made their costumes. Both were witches, and when they were dressed up in their costumes, no one was able to tell them apart.

They also played musical instruments while in elementary school in Helper and then in junior high in California as well. George bought John a violin that he played for a short time; he hated it. George then took the violin away from John and gave it to Nick. Nick liked playing it and continued, taking lessons for several years. John started playing the clarinet, enjoyed it, and played it for many years. The elementary school in Helper had a marching band, and both John and Mike played in the band. In fact, much later, when John entered junior high school in California, he started his own band. Mike started out playing the snare drum and then learned all the percussion instruments in the orchestra. He also played drums in his brother's band.

Terpsihori and George were always proud of their children and loved bragging about them when the opportunity arose. They continued to go to church on Sundays and take part in all the community activities that were offered. Terpsihori helped out and taught in the Greek school set up by the church. Her education in Greece provided a solid background for her, and she was an excellent teacher. The Greeks in this close-knit community tried to instill in their children an appreciation for Greek culture and a sense of pride in their heritage. Both George and Terpsihori were highly thought of, respected, and liked by all.

Greek women helped each other when someone was sick and shared knowledge of folklore medicines, which they had brought with them from Greece. In times of illness, they rallied around each other and never hesitated to help out if necessary. Some of these women had developed a good reputation for curing the sick, and Terpsihori used some of their folklore remedies for her family. One of the remedies she used to treat a bad cold was called "cupping," which involved heating the inside of drinking glasses with a small flame and then plopping the warm glass on the person's back. The warm glass would suck the skin into the glass, and the heat and the suction would draw the toxins out of the person's system.

The boys still remember the ritual they watched as Terpsihori prepared to do this. First, she would get about six empty water glasses and set them down on a table near the bed where her patient was lying, facedown. She would also tear a cloth into strips and wrap the strips of cloth around several forks. She would dip each of the wrapped forks into alcohol and light the cloth with a match. She then quickly picked up a glass with one hand, swirled the burning fork with the other hand on the inside of the glass for a split second, and plopped the glass on the person's back. The patient could have as many as six glasses on his back at one time, and the process would be repeated every several minutes.

This remedy worked for bad colds, flu, and even pneumonia; it was one of many folklore "cures" that the women brought from Greece.

Greek communities in America used these folklore treatments because they had grown up with them in the old country; they were a part of their culture. But from the point of view of American law enforcement agencies, this particular treatment, "cupping," when used on a child, was looked upon as child abuse. It took time, but gradually law enforcement agencies learned that the intent of folklore medicine was to treat and cure, not injure, a child. This knowledge helped to cast a different light on these types of police investigations.

A funny story that was told many times by Terpsihori and George, and even later on by John and Mike themselves, was the story about when the boys were going to have their tonsils removed. John and Mike were having trouble with their tonsils, and the doctor thought it best if they both had them taken out. The doctor gave George and Terpsihori a special price if they would let him remove the boys' tonsils on the same day.

Terpsihori made an appointment for the operations. On the day of the appointment, she and George took John and Mike to the doctor's office for the surgery. The doctor asked the boys who wanted to go in first and offered to flip a coin to see who it would be. Mike spoke up and said that he would go first, and both George and Terpsihori went into the surgery room with him. Mike laid down on the operating gurney, and the doctor prepared him for the operation. The doctor held some gauze over Mike's nose and proceeded to drop ether on it, asking Mike to take deep breaths. The smell of the ether was strong and caused Mike to panic. He started screaming and yelling for them to stop. John had been sitting in the waiting room and, upon hearing Mike's screams, tried to open the door to see what was going on. The door was locked, so he peeked through the keyhole in the door and saw his mother and father trying to hold Mike down while the doctor was trying to put him to sleep with the ether. When John heard the screaming and saw Mike being held down, he believed that they were "killing" his brother. He made up his mind right then and there that he was not going to have his tonsils taken out and ran out of the doctor's office. The doctor finally got Mike to sleep and removed his tonsils.

George and Terpsihori went to get John and found that he was not in the waiting room. They started looking for him and made some inquiries, asking different people if they had seen him. With Helper being such a small town and with everyone knowing each other, it didn't take long to find someone who had seen John running out of the doctor's office just moments earlier. After a while, with everyone looking for him and trying to catch him, John ran into a pregnant woman who grabbed him and held him for Terpsihori and George.

Fighting and yelling, John was taken back to the doctor's office. George thought maybe it wasn't a good idea to operate on John at that time, but the doctor thought otherwise, and persuaded George and Terpsihori to let him take John's tonsils out. After some continued resistance, John was finally put to sleep, and the doctor removed his tonsils. The doctor also cut out the little bell membrane that hangs down at the back of the throat. To this day, John insists that the doctor cut the bell out just to get even with him for giving him such a hard time.

Weeks and months went by, and Terpsihori and George were doing fine. In the spring they had planted a garden in the backyard. The yard was too big to plow by hand, so George borrowed a horse and plow and plowed the yard in a half a day. The boys helped him with the plowing and the planting of the garden.

After a few months, they began to harvest some of the vegetables. There was an abundance of tomatoes, squash, green beans, cucumbers, and a variety of other vegetables. The fruit trees in the yard (apricot, peach, and cherry) were just filled with fruit that had to be picked. Terpsihori, with the help of some friends and her sons, canned a lot of the vegetables and fruit, sharing her canned goods with friends and neighbors.

The basement of the house was an ideal place for George to make wine. He would rent the equipment, which consisted of a large vat and wine barrels. He would buy bushels of grapes and throw the grapes into the large vat. This ritual became a family project. All the family members would take off their shoes and socks, wash their feet, get in the vat and stomp on the grapes until the vat was full of grape juice.

George then filtered the juice from the pulp and poured the grape juice into barrels. He would allow the juice to ferment and turn into wine. When the wine was ready, he opened the spigot and filled a bottle or two for the family to enjoy. A glass of wine was always served at the dinner table, and John and Mike were allowed to have a glass, as long as it was watered down. In actuality, the wine was watered down so much that it had only the coloring and a little taste of wine to it. However, sometimes the wine was not diluted enough, and after a few drinks, the boys would get a little tipsy.

During the summer, the boys would help some of the farmers harvest their crops, and they enjoyed doing it, especially harvesting the alfalfa and hay. While horses would pull the wagons that were used to haul the hay, John and Mike used pitchforks and helped pitch the hay into the wagons. The hay would then be hauled up into the loft of the barn and stored. The boys made a game of working the hay. After all the hay was stored in the barn and their work done, the boys would jump from the loft of the barn onto the hay that was piled up high. No one would get hurt by jumping into it, and the boys spent many wonderful days working the alfalfa fields.

*Terpsihori with her husband George and his sister Eleni in 1929, Crete, Greece*

*Terpsihori (early 20's)   George (early 40's)*

*Terpsihori with John 3 yrs and Mike 1 ½ years Helper, Utah 1933*

*Terpsihori 1945 in San Pedro, California*

*George and Terpsihori with sons Mike, Nick, Chuck & John 1945, San Pedro, California.*

*George and Terpsihori on their 50th Wedding anniversary dinner held on June 29, 1979, Torrance, California*

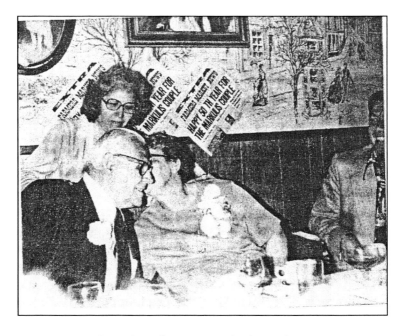

*George and Terpsihori whispering to each other on their anniversity.*

# CHAPTER 15:

# *Mischief-Makers*

One day, John received a spanking from his father, and he got very angry. John heard that some farmers were hiring workers to harvest their crops, and he wanted to get a job so he could earn some money. Without telling anyone, he took off to look for work at the different farms. John met a group of crop pickers who hired him at about twenty-five cents a day plus his room and board. This wasn't bad money for a ten-year-old. Terpsihori got worried because John had never been away from home on his own, and she kept asking Mike if he knew where his brother might be. She knew that Mike and John were inseparable and thought that Mike knew where John had gone. In truth, John had never told Mike what his intentions were, and he kept telling his mother and father that he did not know where John had gone.

Several days had gone by, and still no one knew where John was. After making some inquiries, George learned that John was working some of the farms with a group of crop workers who had taken him in. Taking Mike with him, George borrowed a pickup truck and went to look for his missing son.

After about half a day going from farm to farm, they finally found him. The sun was on the horizon, dusk was settling in, and all the farm workers had quit work for the day. John was living in a small tent with other crop workers. When George saw him, he grabbed him, dragged him to the pickup truck, and gave him a good whipping. George also started yelling at several of the crop workers for taking John on without getting the permission of his parents. As he looked around, he could see that there were many other young boys in the group who also had left home to earn some money. One could only think about what their parents were going through, not knowing where their children were.

George continued scolding John as they drove back home. Terpsihori was relieved that John was now home and safe, but she was also extremely angry and scolded him while she was getting him ready for a bath. He had not taken a bath since he left and was one dirty little boy! As she was bathing him, she told him that if he wanted to work, she would find him a job.

The very next day, Terpsihori went to a Greek friend of their family who owned a candy store across the street from the house. After the owner heard the story of John's attempt to work with the crop workers and realized how upset Terpsihori was, he hired him. The only catch was that John got paid in candy! Of course, Mike, Nick, and Chuck liked the idea because they got to share John's candy.

There were two small movie theaters in Helper about a half block from each other and just down the street from the candy store. The theaters were a short walking distance from the house and often showed really good movies. Some of the favorites were the old gangster movies like *Dillinger* and the old Western cowboy movies with Randolph Scott and John Wayne. Some of the favorite monthly serial-type movies were *Flash Gordon, The Phantom, The Green Hornet, Wild Bill Hickok, Hopalong Cassidy, The Lone Ranger,* and many others. Sometimes the boys would go to the show and see the movie over and over. Sometimes they would fall asleep in the show and be awakened by the manager or, on occasion, by Terpsihori, who would go to the theater looking for her boys.

John and Mike got involved in many other mischievous acts while living in Utah. Remember, John was Mike's idol. He followed him and did whatever John wanted to do and went wherever John wanted to go. This included jumping onto boxcars as the trains went through Helper and riding them for several miles, or standing in front of the trains while the train was coming toward you and then, at the last second or two, jumping off the track. John and Mike also collected railroad explosive caps, which were used by the railroad workers as a caution signal for the trains. The boys got a kick out of throwing rocks at the caps and trying to explode them. A favorite place to do this was on the side of the police station, which just happened to be right next door to the boys' home. They would place the caps on the wall at the side or rear of the police station and throw rocks at the caps. When the rocks hit the caps, a loud explosion would take place. It was a miracle that neither John nor Mike ever got hurt. The police officer working in the station would come running out, looking for whoever was responsible. He suspected that John and Mike were the culprits but could never catch them. On one occasion, John put a bunch of the railroad caps in a gunny sack and tied a rope to the end of the sack. He then swung the rope and let it hit the police station. It exploded, knocked some bricks loose, and put a small hole on the side of the building. The police officer told Terpsihori that he believed her boys were responsible for the vandalism, and if he caught them, he would put them in a reform school. Terpsihori got angry, especially at John, and tried to hit him, but he ran from her. She was so angry at him that she picked up a metal dustpan and threw it at him. It struck him on the back of one of his arms and cut him, and then she bandaged him up. She felt terrible about hurting him but hoped that he had learned a lesson.

During the rainy season, the Price River would rise over the banks and flood the surrounding area for several hundred feet on both sides of the river. The fast-rising current would wash away the wooden bridge that was the connection between the two sides of the river. John and Mike would stand on the bridge and watch the river's current rise, and when it got to the point of washing the bridge away, they would run and jump off. They would then watch the bridge get swept down the river, breaking up in many pieces.

At times, when the bridge was washed away in the current, they got stranded on the opposite side of the river from where they lived. The only way to get back to their side was to walk across a pipe that was about eighteen inches in diameter and ran the full width of the river, about forty feet across. It was dangerous crossing this pipe at any time, but when the river was flooding and the river's current was taking everything in its path, crossing the river on the pipe was treacherous. If one lost his balance and fell off, the river's current would surely carry him away and his life could be lost. But for the boys, invincible at that age, there was a feeling of excitement.

During these heavy rainstorms, when John and Mike had not come home, Terpsihori would worry, knowing that they were exposed to possible harm or injury. Although Terpsihori never found out about some of the things they did, she would still be a nervous wreck because of the rain and the flooding of the river. At times like these, especially in the rainstorms, Mike and John caused her great anxiety. John was the one who got the brunt of the scoldings because he was the oldest and should have known better.

On one hot summer day, John and Mike got into a rock fight with some boys who lived on the other side of Helper. Mike got hit on the forehead, about two inches above his right eye. The rock was thrown hard and cut deep into the skin, with blood spurting from the wound. Mike got scared because he couldn't see with all that blood getting into his eye. John grabbed Mike and they ran home.

Terpsihori panicked when she saw Mike. George happened to be home that day, and he tried to stop the bleeding, but the cut was about three inches long and just wouldn't stop.

Neighbors heard the commotion and came running over to the house. Standing over an open fire in the yard, George took a large knife and held it in the fire until it got red hot. With Terpsihori and a neighbor holding Mike down, George placed the flat blade of the knife on the open wound and cauterized it. The bleeding stopped, but the cauterizing of the wound caused Mike to scream and try to break loose. George and Terpsihori tried to console Mike by telling him that what they did to him was necessary to stop the bleeding, that it would only hurt for a little while, and that he would be all right. Mike's head was bandaged up, and the wound soon healed.

All the boys in the neighborhood were lectured about throwing rocks and how careful they had to be when using their slingshots. Mike could have very easily been hit in the eye and lost his sight. This is one scar that remains with Mike today.

Another incident worthy of mention occurred when a circus had come to town. The circus was always a big thing when it came to Helper, and many of the boys in town would try to get hired setting up the circus. Many times the pay would be free tickets. At several booths at the circus, prizes could be won by breaking bottles with slingshots. The vendors needed lots of bottles and would buy them from the neighborhood children. Mike went out scrounging for bottles and knew that a good place to find them would be at the town dump. While walking through the debris, he stepped into a spot where there was smoldering trash underneath, and he got second and third-degree burns on his left foot. Being in a lot of pain, he immediately ran home. Terpsihori took his shoes and socks off and saw that his left foot was badly blistered; she treated Mike's burns and dressed his foot. It took a while for that foot to heal, and Mike had to spend a lot of time that summer sitting on his front porch. By the way, he missed the circus.

# CHAPTER 16:

# *The Last Move in Helper*

The last home the family lived in prior to moving to California was close to the Price River, and one street separated the Markulis home from the river. The houses on the opposite side of the street, closest to the river, were the ones that always got flooded during bad storms. The families that lived in those homes would have to sweep the mud and water out of their houses whenever the river overflowed. The Markulis home was just far enough away that the water did not reach their house.

All of the people who lived close to the river, but were not affected by the flooding, helped their neighbors with the clean-up process. Among the first to offer were George, Terpsihori, and their sons, showing up with shovels and brooms to help their neighbors in any way they could.

The year 1941 was coming to an end with everyone looking forward to the Christmas holidays. On Sunday, December 7, Terpsihori, George, and all the boys were listening to the radio just as they would on any Sunday morning. Then, the regular programming was interrupted with the unbelievable announcement that Japan had bombed Pearl Harbor and President Roosevelt had declared that the United States was now at war with Japan.

The war caused anxiety for all Americans, including George and Terpsihori. George was fifty-five years old and too old to be drafted. They knew that Europe had been at war with Germany for several years and that Greece was occupied by the Germans. Italy had originally invaded Greece, but the Greek resistance forces defeated the invading Italian army. After a ruthless and brutal battle, Hitler's elite forces and the German army occupied Greece.

George and Terpsihori were concerned for the well-being of their families in Greece. They did not know if they were dead or alive, and there wasn't any way they could find out. They never lost their faith and always believed their families in the old country would survive the war.

Greek families in Greece had to endure great hardship and deprivation throughout the war, which caused bitter resentment toward Italian and German citizens. Some of that resentment was seen in Greek communities in America as well. By presidential decree, Japanese-American citizens living in the United States were taken from their homes and placed in internment camps. Rumors were spread that the government had arrested several Japanese citizens for spying. On the other hand, American citizens of Italian and German decent were not placed in internment camps. In retrospect, it was not only a painful time in American history but also a harsh time. History books and government records now speak of Japanese-Americans "uprooted from their homes, deprived of their property, denied due process, and stripped of their freedom." In 1988, forty-seven years later, the United States officially acknowledged our Country's actions and offered redress to the Japanese.

Helper, in addition to being a coal-mining town, was also a main railroad center. Troop trains and trains loaded with heavy military equipment were now coming through Helper on regular schedules. Seeing the soldiers and military equipment almost on a daily basis brought the reality of the war closer to home.

# CHAPTER 17:

# *The Year Was Now 1942*

Even with all the anxieties of the war and the concern for loved ones in Greece, the Markulis family was doing well. In Helper, as was true all over America, the war created a stronger sense of patriotism. Many young men were getting drafted or enlisting in the service, causing much concern for their safety.

It seemed that everyone got involved in the war effort. The government asked citizens to collect newspapers, scrap metal, old rubber tires, and even old cooking grease. There was also a big push for people to buy savings stamps, which were turned into war bonds. Children would buy stamps with their nickels and dimes and paste them in small folders. When they had bought enough stamps to fill a folder, they would turn it in for a war bond. Everyone was doing their part, adults and children alike. Many items were being rationed, such as sugar, butter, coffee, and gasoline; there were limits on many other items as well. Families were given ration stamps according to the number of people in the family, and they purchased their staples with stamps. It was not unusual for families to trade stamps with each other for certain items.

The boys were doing very well in school. John and Mike were in the fifth grade, Nick was in the second grade, and Chuck had yet to start school. The boys liked school, were very popular, and had many friends. One thing that was nice about living in this particular home was that it was only two blocks from the Helper Elementary School. There were after-school activities that the boys took part in, including a Bible study class in which students received rewards for their learning efforts. One of the awards was a little gold metal fish, approximately half an inch long. It was a challenge to see who would be able to accumulate the most.

Their home had a bench swing on the front porch, and in the evening, the boys would sit on the porch with their friends and tell horror stories. The storyteller had to make up the story as he was telling it, and John was really good at it. He would make up some stories that were really scary, and he would get very dramatic. He knew all the right words and expressions to use and, with the use of a flashlight, did a great job of frightening everyone. Mike, Nick, and Chuck always had a hard time going to sleep after one of John's spooky stories.

Two houses east of the Markulis's residence lived another Greek family. The family had a son named Nicholas, who was about the same age as John and Mike. One night while he was asleep in his bed in one of the back bedrooms, a bullet hit Nicholas in the head. He never knew what hit him, and he never woke up. In the morning his mother went in to awaken him and saw blood on his pillow. She thought he had gotten a nosebleed while he slept, but instead found him dead with a gunshot wound to the head. This was a terrible period for the family to go through and a terrible tragedy to the town of Helper.

Soon, everyone learned what had happened. The rear yards of the houses on this block butted up to the back of the businesses on the main street of Helper. One of the businesses was robbed, and shots were fired during the commission of the crime. One of the bullets ricocheted off a building, went through Nicholas's window, and killed him.

In a coal-mining town, people expected tragedies in the mines to occur, but not tragedies like this that brought such heartbreak and distress to children and their families through criminal behavior. These types of violent acts were seldom seen in the small town of Helper. The Markulis family took Nicholas's death very hard. Terpsihori and George comforted the family and grieved as if the loss was their own.

# CHAPTER 18:

# *George Buys a Coal Mine*

The year 1943 was a dramatic year for the Markulis family. This was to be the last year that Terpsihori, George, and their children were to live in the state of Utah.

As a small child in Crete, George had injured his right eye. Working in the coal mines aggravated the injury; then he re-injured his eye, and glaucoma set in. He was being treated for the disease, but doctors were concerned that if the glaucoma got worse, he would lose the eye. Of course, just working in the mines meant that his good eye could be injured or damaged at any moment. Both George and Terpsihori were devastated by these terrible thoughts, but they decided to wait it out and hope the situation wouldn't get any worse.

The news about the glaucoma came at the same time when things were looking good for the family. George had bought a coal mine and was working from dawn to dusk to make it productive. Terpsihori was giving her husband all the support she could, and John and Mike were going to the mine and helping when they could. To make sure that the boys stayed healthy, Terpsihori would give the boys a tablespoon of cod liver oil every morning; it must have worked, because none of the children got sick. In fact, before she started the boys on the cod liver oil, John had a bad case of asthma, and he believed the cod liver oil cured him of it as well.

George would take John and Mike to the coal mine with him early in the morning, and they would help out with some chores their father had for them to do. Actually, most of the time they played in the mountains until their father quit work at the end of the day. George had a .22-caliber rifle and taught the boys how to shoot it. They would spend hours shooting at rabbits, birds, and targets to pass the time. Terpsihori never liked the idea of her sons shooting the rifle but understood that it was part of growing up in the Rocky Mountains of Carbon County, Utah.

There were times when George would take John and Mike inside the coal mine, but only one at a time to make sure that they wouldn't wander off and get lost. There were many tunnels under the ground.  After being inside for several hours, one's sense of direction could get turned around, and an inexperienced miner could easily get lost.

On one occasion, Mike worked the coal inside a mine shaft with his father. George gave Mike a miner's helmet with a light attached to the front of the helmet. Some of the tunnels were pitch black, and the only means of seeing anything was with the light on the helmet. After several hours in the mine, George asked Mike to lead the way out of the tunnel. Mike started taking his Dad deeper into the mine, at which time George told Mike that he was going the opposite way from the entrance. George then led Mike out of the mine. Mike's sense of direction was completely off. As George was leading the way out, Mike felt as if his dad was going deeper into the mine shaft. The lesson learned was not to go in any mine unless accompanied by an experienced miner. The boys had a lot of respect for their father, and they learned firsthand that a coal miner's job was not only hard work, but dangerous.

The war was still going strong and the allies were now on the offensive, both in Europe and in the Pacific. John, Mike, and Nick, as well as all the children in the community, felt a strong sense of patriotism and played out their feelings in war games. The area around the river became a battlefield with bunkers and trenches. Every war movie that came out seemed to have at least a few battlefield scenes, and the kids would change their riverside battlefields to the configurations they saw in the latest movie. The only problem in playing war games was trying to figure out who was going to be the enemy, as everyone wanted to be on the side of the allies. Everyone wanted to be an American GI in combat.

John Wayne, Clark Gable, Errol Flynn, Robert Taylor, and the many movie stars who portrayed war heroes were emulated. The battlefield around the river was the playground for Helper's children and it seemed that all of their spare time was spent right there on this battlefield. The kids would go to great efforts to make their battleground look realistic, at least in their own minds. Booby traps were set, machine gun nests were set up, and camouflage was replicated as seen in the movies. There was no doubt that a young generation of patriotic kids were training to make themselves available to their country if the need should ever arise.

With Helper being both a railroad center and a coal-mining town, troop trains could be seen on a daily basis going through the town, loaded with soldiers, tanks, and artillery weapons. The trains traveled east and west to destinations unknown to us, from which the troops and equipment would be shipped to the European or the Pacific fronts.

Many of the troop trains would stop in Helper to get fuel, but it was usually a short layover, sometimes only a half hour. Kids would run up to the trains and wave to the soldiers as they passed through. When there was a layover, soldiers often would ask the kids to buy them candy, cigarettes, or things that they needed because the soldiers themselves were not allowed to get off.

On many of the occasions John, Mike, and Nick would try to help and run to the closest store to make some purchases. Many soldiers appreciated the gesture and would give a small tip for their help. Sometimes, when there were too many orders and the wait was too long, kids would run back to the train, give the soldier his money back, and apologize. Other times, the train would pull out and leave while the kids were running back to the train, and they would end up with the merchandise and the change. And, unfortunately, some kids would deliberately wait for the train to pull out and then make a pretense of trying to catch up with it. They would pocket the unspent money.

# CHAPTER 19:

# *George Leaves for Los Angeles*

George's eye was not getting any better; in fact, he could no longer see out of it. The doctors told George he would have to have the eye removed. At that time, doctors had been taught that if someone in George's condition did not have the operation, there was a strong possibility that glaucoma could affect the other eye and the patient would go blind.

George and Terpsihori knew that they had no choice; the eye would have to be removed, and the doctors who were treating George made arrangements for him to go to Los Angeles for the operation. Terpsihori called a Greek friend, Mrs. Evangelia Louros, who lived in San Pedro, California, and explained the situation to her and her husband, Tony. The Louroses reached out, knowing George would need a place to stay while he was recuperating.

George took John with him, and the whole family gave them a send-off at the Greyhound bus station. Watching the bus drive off until it could no longer be seen left Terpsihori with an empty feeling. For the second time in their marriage, she was separated from her husband and again left with the three boys, Mike, Nick, and Chuck. This was very difficult for her, as she wanted to be with George during the surgery, and she knew she couldn't. This separation brought her many tears and many prayers, as she prayed for him every day they were apart. Terpsihori knew this separation was going to be for a short time. She did not know she would be joining her husband in California, instead of George returning to Utah.

George and John took the bus to Los Angeles and then a streetcar to San Pedro. They were met by Tony Louros and his son, Mike, who took them to their home. The Louros family were gracious hosts. George and Mr. and Mrs. Louros reminisced about Greece and the coal-mining towns of Utah. Mrs. Louros, as a young lady in Crete, had worked as a seamstress. In fact, she did a lot of sewing for one of George's sisters. Tony Louros had come to the United States from Crete in 1912, the same year that George made his first trip. They both worked the coal mines in Utah from 1912 to 1929, and both men were on the same ship going back to Crete in 1929 to get married. Both marriages had been arranged and had had contracts drawn up by their families. They were married a week apart from each other, and both couples went back to the United States, with George and Terpsihori leaving a month before Mr. and Mrs. Louros. They went back to Utah and settled down. Mr. Louros later moved his family to San Pedro, where he went into the restaurant business. With all these coincidences in their lives, they had a lot to talk about, as they knew many of the same people.

The eye surgery was successful, and there were no complications. George wore a patch over the right eye socket while he was being fitted with a prosthesis, a glass eye, that would match the shape and color of his other eye. It was amazing how closely the artificial eye resembled his good eye. When it was fitted into the eye socket, it looked exactly like his good eye and moved as a normal eye would. George was pleased with the outcome of the operation and the fitting of the prosthesis.

George stayed in contact with his wife by phone and kept her abreast of the operation and his progress. During one of the conversations, Terpsihori learned that Tony Louros owned a small café on the waterfront in San Pedro and that he had offered her husband a job as a night cook.

George told Terpsihori that he didn't especially like the idea of going back into the coal mines with only one good eye. At fifty-seven years old, George figured he would be able to work in the mines for only a few more years. He felt that this would be a good transition for him and his family. He believed that eventually he could buy a small café of his own.

George convinced Terpsihori. He went on to tell her that San Pedro was a beautiful small town where the Pacific Ocean was within walking distance. He told her how much they would feel closer to their beloved Greece by being so close to the ocean. He described San Pedro's harbor, where ships from all over the world would come and go. Terpsihori could visualize her town of Piraeus, also a major seaport in Greece, and ships from Greece visiting San Pedro's harbor. As he described the beautiful ocean to her, she began to feel homesick for Greece and her family.

Little did she know that some years later, in 1951, she would take a journey of her own, with her then youngest son, Jimmy, and return to Greece for a six-month visit. She had made many friends among the ship hands who worked on the merchant marine ships that came to San Pedro, and they arranged for her to travel with Jimmy on board one of those ships.

George went on to tell her of the many Greek families who lived in San Pedro and the surrounding cities. Terpsihori was excited and at the same time apprehensive about moving to California. The family had established roots in Utah with many dear friends and relatives now residing in Helper, Price, and Salt Lake City. The move would be very difficult for the whole family. It would be strenuous for her boys, as they would be leaving a school that they liked and many friends. They would be starting all over again in a new town, going to a new school, and having to make new friends.

Terpsihori was worried about where they were going to live and what she was going to do with all her furniture. She couldn't help thinking back to her prior moves - to Pennsylvania, and then back to Utah - and the difficult time she had making those transitions. As difficult as it had been, she had managed then and knew she could do it again. What she couldn't take with her, she would sell or give away. Many of the nice things she treasured she would give to special friends and relatives. Other items, having symbolic meaning to her, she would package and leave with friends so they could mail them to her later when she got settled. Through prayer and faith in her husband, Terpsihori knew he was doing the right thing and everything would work out.

During the next few weeks, while Terpsihori worked very hard to make the move and transition go as smoothly as possible, George was looking for a house to rent in San Pedro. He had already started working at Tony Louros's restaurant, Harbor Coney Island Café. He worked with Tony for several days so that Tony could show him the operation of the business. The menu was simple, consisting of breakfasts, hamburgers, hotdogs, chili beans, and steaks. George was already a good cook and took to the work without any problems. George knew he would do a good job.

Through a local San Pedro realtor and with the help of Mr. and Mrs. Louros, George found a nice two-bedroom house in the Barton Hill district of San Pedro. There was an elementary school only one block away where the boys could go to school. For the first time since coming to the United States, George had saved enough for a small down payment and was able to buy his first home. He had lived in the United States for thirty-one years and had purchased three or four cars but never a home. All the homes he and his family lived in had been rented. George was very excited about this new home and the new job and couldn't wait to tell Terpsihori about the house.

Terpsihori, upon hearing the good news, was thrilled that everything was working out. George had also told her that he had been able to keep some of the furniture that was in the house when he bought it. It was not an easy chore to look for furniture, as she recalled from her moves to Pennsylvania and then back again to to Utah. She appreciated George's efforts to make the move easier for her and the boys.

The next few weeks seemed to drag by as she sold or gave away all the belongings that she couldn't take with her. She had a hard time telling her friends that she was moving to California. The entire Greek community, including those from Helper, Price, and the adjoining towns, rallied around Terpsihori and told her that the move was the best thing for her and her husband. They understood that with the loss of one eye, George needed to preserve the sight of his other eye, and continuing to work in the mines would be dangerous. The boys were sad but also the envy of many of their friends because of the move to California. Everyone knew that was where Hollywood was and where all the movies were made!

# CHAPTER 20:

# *Terpsihori and the Children Leave for California*

Terpsihori contacted her cousin, George Galanis, in Salt Lake City and told him of the move. He wanted to see her before she left for California, as did other friends and relatives in Salt Lake. She wanted to see them as well, and so she decided that she would visit them on her way to California.

Terpsihori bought bus tickets from Helper to Salt Lake City for herself and the three boys. When the bus pulled out of the bus depot in Helper, Terpsihori started to cry, and Mike, being the oldest on the trip, tried to console her, as did Nick and Chuck. Looking at her sons, Terpsihori was amazed at how much they had grown. Mike was now twelve, Nick was ten, and Chuck was six. She hugged her sons and wondered where the years had gone. She also told her sons everything was going to be fine and the family was going to like California. She even went on to tell them about Greece and how much California resembled her country. The trip to Salt Lake City didn't seem to take very long, as Terpsihori occupied the time by telling her sons about when she was growing up in Greece, including stories about her mother, father, brother, and sisters. The boys never recalled her talking as much about her beloved Greece as she did on this trip. Tears welled up in her eyes when she was remembering those times and talking about her family and the old country. Nick and Chuck hugged her, and Mike told her that someday she would get to see them again. Terpsihori smiled at Mike, returned the hug, and said she knew she would.

For the first time, the boys had a better understanding of how their parents felt, missing their families and country of birth as much as they did. Mike tried to imagine his parents growing up in Greece, but there were no childhood pictures of them in Greece, so Terpsihori's stories were of people and places with which he and his brothers could not easily identify. They certainly knew they had grown up in the small Greek communities of Utah and Pennsylvania, but Terpsihori's stories sounded wonderful, as she romanticized her beautiful country. The boys told their mother that someday they wanted to see Greece and the places where she and their father had grown up. Within the next fifty years, four of her sons visited and saw the same beauty and majesty of the Greek islands that she had seen so long ago.

When they arrived at the bus station in Salt Lake City, they were met by Terpsihori's cousin, George Galanis. He was close to Terpsihori's age, was legally blind, had mastered the English language, and operated a small sundries store. His pleasant personality made Terpsihori and her sons feel welcome. George lived in a hotel, where he rented a room, and it was within walking distance of the bus station, so George and the boys each grabbed a piece of luggage and walked to his hotel.

It was obvious that something was wrong because even though it was two in the afternoon, only a few people could be seen on the streets. It was an eerie feeling, as if the whole city had been deserted. Cousin George explained that the whole city had been hit hard with a polio epidemic and that the entire city was practically quarantined because hundreds of adults and children had contracted the disease. This caused Terpsihori to worry, and she knew her stay in Salt Lake City would be a short one. During this period in Utah's history, polio was called the "loathsome killer of Utah's youth."

Terpsihori arranged for her and her boys to meet with some of her relatives the next day. This took some time because the families they were to visit lived in different parts of the city. While they went to meet the relatives, their cousin George went to the train station and purchased tickets for the family to travel on to Los Angeles.

At one of the homes that Terpsihori and the boys visited that day, they saw the scourge of polio firsthand. A young boy, maybe ten or eleven years old, was in an iron lung. The boy laid in this large cylindrical device, with only his head sticking out at one end, and it did his breathing for him. It was keeping the boy alive.

Polio usually struck in the summer. Children who were frolicking and playing one day lay motionless the next day in polio's fevered grip. The word "polio" conjured heartrending images of children in leg braces and iron lungs. If one didn't die from it, it left the person paralyzed. Thank God, some years later Dr. Jonas Salk, along with another researcher, Albert Sabin, developed a vaccine for this terrible disease. By the mid-1960s, polio was virtually eradicated in the United States, but only after it had taken its toll on the lives of thousands of victims and their families.

The sight of the young polio victim in the iron lung had a tremendous impact on Terpsihori and her sons. She wanted to leave Salt Lake City and take her sons away from the terrible wrath of this disease.

Cousin George had purchased the train tickets for the following day. The trip would take about eighteen hours to reach Los Angeles, because there were several stops that the train had to make on the way. Terpsihori and the boys were anxious to leave Salt Lake and to be reunited with the rest of the family.

Cousin George was extremely helpful, gave Terpsihori a lot of good advice, and made her promise that she would write to him. Being cousins, being family, meant a lot to both of them. He was a wonderful man and an extraordinary person. Although he was considered legally blind, it never kept him from being a productive citizen in his community. He was a cantor in the Greek Orthodox Church and helped out whenever he could. His glasses were very thick, and he could see objects if he put them up close to his eyes. He earned enough through his sundries store to live comfortably. At the time of Terpsihori's visit, he was single, but he got married years later to a lovely woman whom he met at a therapy session for the blind. She was one of the counselors who worked with people who were blind or going blind.

Cousin George took Terpsihori and the boys to the train station in the late afternoon, and he bought the boys some candy and cookies for them to eat on the trip. Good-byes were said, the family boarded the train, they found that they had very nice accommodations, and they made themselves comfortable. The train had a dining car and regular-size bathrooms. Their assigned seats converted into bunk beds at night. Each car had a conductor who catered to the passengers. This experience definitely was unlike any of the bus trips they had taken in the past. They later learned that their cousin George had paid an additional cost for these nice accommodations without telling Terpsihori. His generosity was really appreciated, as it made the trip much more pleasant.

The train had a lot of passengers, of whom many were military personnel, soldiers and sailors who were going to Los Angeles because they had shipping orders for overseas. Some of the military personnel, along with other passengers, would get off the train at one of the several stops on the way, including Las Vegas, Nevada. In 1943, Las Vegas was not much of a metropolis; in fact, Terpsihori and the boys had never heard of it.

The train ride was a wonderful treat, and the boys enjoyed watching the countryside as the train slowly traveled on its rails. There was always something new and different to see, because the landscape took on many different colors and shapes as they continued on their trip. One minute you would be traveling through a residential community, and the next moment the train was climbing a mountain or going through tunnels. Even a twelve-year-old like Mike could understand how difficult it must have been to build the railroad system across the United States. Living in Helper, a small coal-mining town and railroad center, the boys had never thought about what railroads really meant to this country until they took this particular train ride and experienced it firsthand. They were enjoying their trip. When dinnertime came, they went into the dining car, sat down at a table, and ordered from a menu. Terpsihori ordered hot turkey sandwiches, which were served open-faced with mashed potatoes and gravy. The dinner was delicious, and it even came with dessert!

The boys went to bed early, as they wanted to try out the bunk beds. But they ended up talking half the night. They were anxious about moving so far from Utah, not knowing anyone, having to go to a new school, and making new friends. They finally fell asleep, listening to the train as it rode the rails.

In the morning, Terpsihori woke them up and made sure they were washed up and neatly dressed, because they would be arriving in Los Angeles in a few hours. She took the boys to the dining car for breakfast. Everyone had scrambled eggs, toast, and milk. Mike thought the scrambled eggs were particularly delicious. He never forgot how good the eggs were, and many years later he perfected his own version of what he had eaten on that trip. To this day, when he makes scrambled eggs for his children and grandchildren, he fondly remembers the eggs he ate on that trip. They were that good.

The train finally arrived at Union Station in Los Angeles. The train station was enormous and beautiful, with a lot of activity as passengers arrived and departed. Mike knew many movies had been filmed in that station, and he was standing right there, watching everything going on around him!

Terpsihori was now concerned about catching the right bus to San Pedro. After the boys made some inquiries, they were directed to the place where they could catch the Greyhound bus to San Pedro. It was in the late afternoon, and Terpsihori telephoned George at the Louros residence. Terpsihori left a message with Mr. Louros that she and the boys had arrived in Los Angeles, and she gave him the time that their bus would be arriving in San Pedro.

# CHAPTER 21:

# *Terpsihori's Life in California*

Life in California was so dramatically different from that in Utah or Pennsylvania. The demographics changed from coal-mining towns and Rocky Mountains to a suburban lifestyle, with a population density much larger than what the family had previously experienced. George had bought a home in Barton Hill, which was in one of the lower-income areas of San Pedro.

Terpsihori fell in love with San Pedro, as she found herself close to the ocean and could easily reminisce about her home by the Aegean Sea. It did not take Terpsihori long to get settled in her new home, and she found that there were many old friends and acquaintances living in San Pedro whom she knew from Greece. She also made many new friends, and her neighbors took a liking to her. They would visit each other quite often, which improved her English. When she was not comfortable talking in English, she would have the boys interpret for her.

Close to their home was a small grocery store where she would go for some of her shopping or send one of her boys to buy an item or two. The war was still in progress, and you could buy certain items only with ration stamps. People found themselves trading with or even buying stamps from each other.

There was no Greek Orthodox Church in the area, and she had to take the streetcar to the the church in Los Angeles. Not too many Greek families owned automobiles, and they used public transportation extensively, especially the Barton Hill bus line, which had a stop one block from their home. For a nickel, one could take the bus to downtown San Pedro and even obtain a transfer to go to any other part of San Pedro.

The education system for the boys was very different. In Utah, children would spend a whole year in one grade, but in California, there were "A" semesters and "B" semesters. There was some confusion regarding Mike's age, so instead of going into the sixth grade as he would have in Utah, he had to start school in grade "A-5," thus losing half a semester. John went to Cabrillo Avenue School because he continued to use the Louros family's address. Mike, Nick, and Chuck were enrolled in Barton Hill Elementary School.

All the boys did well in school, getting good grades. When the boys graduated from their elementary schools, they went on to Henry Dana Junior High School, which was a little over a mile from their home in Barton Hill. The boys continued to do well in school, winning prestigious awards and, upon graduating from junior high school, John and Mike each received the American Legion Award. All the boys held student offices while in junior high, and Mike was elected student body president. All of the boys were also involved in athletics, which would become even more meaningful as they went on to high school and college.

John worked at a variety of jobs while in junior high school, including at a grocery store, dress shop, the naval shipyard, and DiCarol's Bakery. Mike had a paper route, delivering the *San Pedro News Pilot*; he also took John's place at the dress shop when John left to work at DiCarlo's Bakery. Eventually, Mike and Nick also went to work at DiCarlo's, with Chuck doing the same later on.

George worked at Tony Louros's restaurant, Harbor Coney Island Café, on the waterfront in San Pedro, working the night shift from 9:00 p.m. to 7:00 a.m. George was always a hard worker, and he had become an outstanding cook. He almost never took a day off except on Christmas Day. Everyone who came to the restaurant loved his food. All who came in contact with George admired him, including servicemen, soldiers, sailors, merchant seamen, longshoremen, and port workers. Seamen, no matter where they were from, had heard of George's cooking in San Pedro and would make sure to stop in and have a meal. He never turned a seaman away, even when one didn't have any money; he would give him a free meal. George would not hesitate to feed any hungry or homeless person who came to his restaurant. He was well remembered for being a kind and generous man.

Over time, George opened several small restaurants on the waterfront in San Pedro, finally retiring in his late eighties. The last restaurant he owned, George's Café, was taken over by the City, and all the buildings on that part of the waterfront, including the restaurant, were torn down for the redevelopment of the port.

San Pedro, was home to an army camp, Fort MacArthur. Italian prisoners of war were housed there. On one occasion, Terpsihori was taking her son, Mike, to catch the bus and do some shopping in downtown San Pedro. Holy Trinity Catholic Church was across the street from the bus stop, and the army happened to take the Italian prisoners to Mass at that church. Upon seeing the prisoners, Terpsihori got angry, because she knew that Italy had invaded Greece during the war and had killed and wounded many Greek citizens. Mike had never seen his mother get that angry. She started picking up rocks and was going to throw the rocks at the prisoners. Mike stopped her and convinced her that she would get in trouble. It took her the rest of the day to settle down.

Many of Terpsihori's friends and relatives suffered as a result of the war. She was proud the Italians lost the war with Greece, and it took Hitler's elite troops to conquer their country. Greeks felt a lot of animosity and hatred toward the Italians and Germans for what they did to their beloved country.

# CHAPTER 22:

# *Terpsihori Gives Birth to Her Fifth Son*

As time went on, Terpsihori found herself pregnant and thought that there was still a possibility her dream of having a little girl would come true. On September 17, 1947, her new baby was born in San Pedro, California. To her surprise and disappointment, she had another boy. A beautiful boy! As the story goes in our family, when he was born, Terpsihori told the doctor to put him back, as she did not want another boy. But she loved Dimitri George Markulis just as much as her other sons, if not more. The English translation for Dimitri was James, and he quickly became known as Jimmy.

Terpsihori had wanted a girl so badly she dressed Jimmy up in girls' clothing and let his hair grow long. Jimmy had beautiful long curly hair. The boys, like their mother, also spoiled Jimmy. By now, in 1947, John was seventeen, Mike was sixteen, Nick was fourteen, and Chuck was ten.

Time seemed to move by rather quickly. John and Mike were in high school, with Nick and Chuck in junior high school. Being an outstanding athlete, John played football. In his freshman year on the San Pedro High School football team, he cracked a vertebra and was put in a plaster body cast from his neck down to his groin area. For a while, he was one miserable young man. The doctor had told him that he would never play football again. When his body cast came off, John went out for varsity football and made first-string right guard. John played football for two more years, making first-string all-league. John also excelled in high school, holding leadership positions and, because he was an articulate speaker and quick thinker, winning several speech debates and competitions.

Mike also went out for varsity football and baseball while in high school. He did well, as did Nick and Chuck when they got to high school, both excelling in football. Chuck made first-string all-city fullback. Both boys went on to college and played football, Nick at the University of Oregon and Chuck at Everett Community College in the state of Washington. Chuck continued to excel in the sport, making all-American at the community college level. All the Markulis boys did well in high school, getting good grades and holding prestigious offices, to which they were elected by the student body. George and Terpsihori were proud of their sons, as they not only did well in school but also continued to work, helping out the family.

In June of 1950, the Korean War had broken out and President Truman committed troops to the conflict. John was drafted into the army and served while seeking a deferment. He was nineteen, was married to Anita Mcguinness, and they already had their first baby. He wanted to be sure his family was being taken care of, and so he asked for and received a discharge and deferment from the army.

Upon Mike's graduation from high school in January 1951, he was also drafted. He finished his basic training at Fort Ord, California, and got shipped out to Korea for eighteen months. While he was waiting to get shipped out in Pittsburg, California, Terpsihori took her toddler son, Jimmy, and went to the base, demanding to see the commanding officer. In her broken English, she somehow convinced the command staff that it was important for her to see the commanding officer. Mike was summoned to the office and was asked if he knew the woman who was there. Mike told the CO that she was his mother and the little boy was his brother. Terpsihori tried to convince the CO not to send her son to Korea. After the CO and Mike talked to her for a while, Terpsihori left and returned to San Pedro. She had not wanted her son to be in Korea, in harm's way, and this was a true reflection of the love she had not only for her son Mike, but for all her children.

The year of 1951 was a year full of memorable stories for the family. One such story stands out. When Jimmy was about four years old, sprouting that beautiful long, curly hair, his brother John got tired of his mother trying to raise Jimmy like a girl. Unbeknownst to Terpsihori, John took Jimmy to the local barbershop and told the barber to cut Jimmy's hair and give him a "little boy's haircut." The barber hesitated. John told the barber to cut Jimmy's hair, and that is what the barber did. John asked the barber to put Jimmy's cut hair in a paper bag for him. John then took Jimmy home, gave him the bag of hair, and told him to go in the house and give the bag to his mother. Terpsihori, upon seeing Jimmy without his long, curly hair, got very angry. John was smart enough not to stay at the house after he took Jimmy home! The family talked about this episode for many years.

# CHAPTER 23:

# *Terpsihori Returns to Greece in 1951*

As the years went by, Terpsihori learned that the *San Pedro News Pilot* published a list of the ships coming into the harbor, with their port of origin. Whenever she recognized the Greek merchant ships coming into the port of San Pedro, she would make an effort to contact the Greek seamen and invite them to the house for dinner. Many seamen came for dinner, appreciated having a good homemade Greek meal, and were surprised how many of the same families they knew from Greece. Terpsihori, prior to coming to the United States, had lived in Piraeus, the port city at Athens.

It was through her contacts with the Greek seamen that she made arrangements to take a trip back to Greece in 1951 aboard one of the merchant ships. After twenty-two years in America, and with George's blessings and encouragement, she returned to Greece and stayed for about six months. She visited family and friends whom she had not seen in so many long years. The visit fulfilled her dream of seeing Greece again and she hoped that one day she could return once more. Indeed, in the 1980s, her sons treated their parents to a vacation in Greece.

On this 1951 trip she took her four-year-old son, Jimmy, who could not speak much Greek at the time. He understood everything but could not speak the language. After their six-month stay, Terpsihori returned to the United States. Jimmy had now forgotten all his English, spoke only Greek, and astonished his family and friends at how fluent he was in the language.

During this same period, Mike was in Korea, stationed in Pusan. One morning, Mike had to make a run into downtown Pusan. He was driving a Jeep, and on the way he saw four Greek soldiers walking along the highway. Mike pulled up alongside them and asked them if they would like a ride. When they got in the Jeep, Mike began talking to them in Greek. They were surprised and proud that this American soldier was speaking Greek with them. Mike told them that he was a Greek-American, and his parents had been born in Greece. Mike told them where he was stationed, invited them to his base, and they became friends. Mike told them that his mother, Terpsihori, was in Greece as they spoke, and she was visiting her family in Piraeus. These soldiers had been on the front lines for a year and were now being rotated back to Greece. They were scheduled to enter the port of Piraeus, and they told Mike that when they got back, they would try to locate his mother. Based on just the information Mike provided, they located the Galanis family and found Mike's mother. Terpsihori was surprised and elated that these Greek soldiers had met her son in Korea. They assured her that Mike was all right and not in harm's way from the war.

CHAPTER 24:

# The Family through the Decades

The majority of the Markulis family remained in San Pedro, California, over the next six-plus decades. Here is a glimpse of that journey.

### John, the "Bread Man" and Philanthropist

In 1951, John was discharged from the army and went back to work at DiCarlo's Bakery. Over the next few years, he demonstrated that he was an outstanding employee and found himself getting promoted to supervisory positions. He was eventually placed in charge of the sales department, and John became a vital part of the sales operation at DiCarlo's. Continental Baking Company then purchased DiCarlo's, and John knew his future with Continental was uncertain.

At the same time, Puritan Bakery, a small family bakery located in Santa Monica, California, was losing customers and was in financial trouble. The owner, Dwight Grimes, had recently passed away, and his son, Tom Grimes, became the owner of Puritan. Tom knew that he and the company were in dire need of someone or something to help bring the bakery through this financial crisis and get it back to being profitable. He knew that John, as head of DiCarlo's sales department, was one of the main reasons Puritan had been losing customers. Tom decided he had a potential solution. He telephoned John and asked if he would meet with him. During that meeting, Tom asked John to come over to Puritan, and he offered John a full partnership in the Puritan Baking Company. After talking to his family about this proposal, John accepted Tom Grimes's offer.

Over the next five-plus decades, the partnership between John and Tom Grimes created a dynasty, with Puritan Bakery as a multi-million-dollar operation. John was a highly respected businessman in the baking industry. His reputation as an honest businessman and a philanthropist, especially among his Greek customers, earned him the name "*Yiannis O Psomas*," a respectful phrase meaning "John the Bread Man." John, like his father before him, would never hesitate to help any of his Greek customers if they were in financial difficulty. Every Greek Orthodox Church in the county of Los Angeles could rely on John to help them with their Greek festivals, raising money for their churches. Because of John's leadership, Puritan Bakery was highly praised and recognized by many community organizations for its generous contributions.

Over these five decades, John and Anita's family grew, welcoming four children: Lorraine, George, Cathy, and John John (JJ). All of them have professional careers, enjoy the work they do, and, like their father, give back to their communities. Today, their family is blessed with thirteen grandchildren and two great-grandchildren.

John passed away in 2014 at the age of eighty-three after a long and valiant battle with pneumonia and other health issues. The Puritan Bakery's customers, friends, and employees showed their respect and admiration when several thousand attended his services. This was a wonderful tribute and send-off to John, who was a legend in his own right, from a young, mischievous boy to the loved philanthropist and businessman he became.

## *Mike, the Police Officer and College Professor*

Mike, upon being discharged from the army, also went back to work at DiCarlo's Bakery. While working at the bakery, he married his childhood sweetheart, Alicia Sanchez, and they were together fifty-five years before her passing.

In 1956, Mike left the bakery and joined the Los Angeles Police Department. While at the bakery and during his early years on the police department, he continued his education, graduating from Los Angeles Harbor College and from the California State University at Long Beach.

He was on the Los Angeles Police Department for thirty-seven years, rising to the rank of Lieutenant II, and serving as commanding officer of several detective divisions, including homicide. While in the department, he was employed for thirty years as a part-time instructor in the Community College District of Los Angeles. He taught police science and administration of justice classes at East Los Angeles College and Los Angeles Harbor College.

Mike was recognized on numerous occasions throughout his law enforcement career by LAPD, the universities for which he worked, and community groups for his on and off-duty contributions. He helped establish the Gang Alternatives Program (GAP), which has impacted thousands of elementary school children through the Los Angeles Unified School District and in several independent school districts. He continues to be active in the community today and still serves on the GAP Board. He received many commendations and citations, which included ones for bravery in several sensitive situations.

Upon retiring from the police department in 1992, he took a position with the University of Southern California (USC) as Director of the Delinquency Control Institute, under the School of Public Administration.

Early in their marriage, Mike and Alicia welcomed two children into their family, Elaine and Mark. Both prospered in their respective fields and, like their parents, support community and church activities. Mike continues to enjoy their three grandchildren, who have always brought joy and happiness into his life.

## Nick, the Teacher and Entrepreneur

Nick graduated from the University of Oregon and became a schoolteacher, teaching in Oregon and California. Nick applied for and accepted a teaching position with the federal government. He then became a school teacher with the US Air Force, teaching high school classes to children of military families in Japan. After a two-year tour there, he accepted a teaching position in Germany, again teaching children of military families. Nick returned to the United States and resumed his teaching career in California.

Nick was outgoing, made contacts easily, and had unique opportunities in public relations. Nick also became a proficient golfer. At one time in his career, he combined those two abilities and coordinated golf tournaments to raise funds for charities. He was successful, became well known, and was soon offered a public relations position with an engineering company. Later, Nick used his experience in public relations by going into the publishing business, focusing on sales. He published several real estate magazines, such as the *Home Buyer's Guide*, and newspapers, advertising restaurants in Southern California.

Nick is retired and lives with his wife, Nina, in the Sacramento area of California.

## Chuck, the Music Man and Owner of "Hard Times Family Billiards"

In high school and his early years in college, Chuck had the potential of being one of the country's greatest football players. He excelled in the sport, made all-city at San Pedro High School, and was sought after by many colleges and universities throughout California and other states. He chose the University of Washington, which sent him to Everett Junior College in Everett, Washington. While there, he took regular classes and played football, again demonstrating his outstanding abilities as a football player. Chuck made the junior college All-America list.

Although he loved football and his college years, he became interested in music, and it soon became his passion. He chose to leave college and pursued a career in the music business. He produced several hit records, including "Love You So" and "My Babe" by Ron Holden. These two songs spent several weeks at the number one spot on the Billboard chart. Chuck went on to form his own labels, "R&B" and "Nite Owl Records," which launched the careers of doo-wop stars, the Gallards, and Seattle's top-ten hit maker, Ron Holden.

When Chuck decided to move on from the music business, he returned to San Pedro, where he married his high school sweetheart, Marquita.

Always looking for new and interesting business-related projects, Chuck then turned to the restaurant business. He, his brothers John and Nick, and their father, George, opened up a restaurant in Garden Grove, California. After several successful years, they sold the business.

Chuck and Marquita had one son, Michael. Tragically, Marquita died following a horrific, motorcycle accident.

Following Marquita's passing, Chuck and his son opened a series of family billiard halls, called Varsity and Hard Times. Over many years, they eventually sold them all, except the one they built in Sacramento, California. The world-renowned Hard Times Family Billiards establishment holds annual national and international tournaments with some of the world's best players. Chuck Markulis's name is well known throughout the billiard tournament circles. He supported charities and donated to educational programs in the area. He was well liked and respected.

In spring of 2008, Chuck was involved in a terrible incident in the Hard Times parking lot. He was struck by a vehicle, fell down, hit his head on the pavement, and went into a coma. Although Chuck regained consciousness, he remained hospitalized for months. The damage was severe. He eventually slipped back into a coma and died in June 2008. His family misses him.

## Jimmy, the Baker and Restaurant/Bar Owner

Jim was a good student all through school. His gregarious personality made him one of the most popular students in San Pedro High School. He always joked around and made everyone laugh. Jim played varsity football. He later formed a slow-pitch softball team in San Pedro and played in many tournaments, winning several championships.

Jim decided on a career in the bakery business. He left DiCarlo's Bakery to take a supervisory position with the Puritan Baking Company, where he worked throughout his career. After forty-five years in the baking industry, he retired from Puritan.

During all those years he worked at Puritan, Jimmy also developed his own businesses by opening and operating several bars in San Pedro. He was an excellent businessman and well liked by all who met him. Like his father before him and his brother, John, Jimmy would always be sure that anyone who came in but didn't have the money to pay was offered something to eat.

Jim married his high school sweetheart, Carmela Lauro. They had two beautiful daughters, Alexis and Cynthia. After many years, his marriage ended in divorce. In September, 2006, Jim married Debbie Armstrong and became a stepfather to Stephanie and Sholeh. Jim is also the grandfather to two beautiful granddaughters.

# Afterword

Terpsihori and George lived full lives, raising a family through some of the most difficult times in the history of the United States and the world. George, born in 1886, and Terpsihori, born in 1907, lived through World War I, World War II, and the Korean and Vietnam conflicts. They raised a family in the shanty coal-mining towns of Utah and Pennsylvania and did so through the Depression years. Terpsihori, through a contract marriage arranged by her family and George's family, believed she was marrying a rich Greek coal miner. Instead, she found herself in total disbelief, having left the good life afforded to her by her family in Greece for the godforsaken Rocky Mountains of Utah.

Terpsihori's struggle made her a legend, and her life could easily be written in the history books of immigrants coming to the United States, working hard, raising a family and, through difficult times, successfully achieving the American dream. Not rich, but comfortable, she raised a family with her best ingredients of love, compassion, and empathy, not only for her family but for all with whom she came in contact.

Many stories of immigrants have been written about men and the hardships they endured trying to assimilate into the American dream. Terpsihori's story is about a beautiful young Greek lady who could have lived a life of plenty within the beautiful surroundings of the Greek Islands and the Aegean Sea. Rather than doing so, she chose a life in a new land with a man more than twenty years her senior, whom she did not know, except for a short courtship, as a result of a custom where marriages were arranged by their families. However, her destiny was laid out for her, and she persevered in seeking a life that brought her happiness, joy, sadness, and a full life of contentment with many children, grandchildren, and great-grandchildren. Her story is a true-life storybook adventure that should be told and read by all to show that dreams can and do come true.

*Terpsihori and George with their five sons. Chuck missing from the collage.*
*Below: Nick, Chuck, Mike, John and Jim*

*Mischief-makers who made this story possible. Brothers.*
*John (age 83); Mike (age 82). 2013.*